With joy!

Molly

Chappell

A Vineyard
Garden

A Vineyard Garden

IDEAS FROM THE EARTH
FOR GROWING, COOKING, DECORATING,
AND ENTERTAINING

MOLLY CHAPPELLET

FOREWORD BY HUGH JOHNSON
PAINTINGS BY LYGIA CHAPPELLET
DESIGN BY JACQUELINE JONES DESIGN

VIKING
STUDIO
BOOKS

VIKING STUDIO BOOKS

Published by the Penguin Group

Viking Penguin, a division of Penguin Books USA Inc.,

375 Hudson Street, New York, New York 10014, U.S.A.

Penguin Books Ltd, 27 Wrights Lane,

London W8 5TZ, England

Penguin Books Australia Ltd, Ringwood,

Victoria, Australia

Penguin Books Canada Ltd, 10 Alcorn Avenue, Suite 300,

Toronto, Ontario, Canada M4V 3B2

Penguin Books (N.Z.) Ltd, 182-190 Wairau Road,

Auckland 10, New Zealand

Penguin Books Ltd, Registered Offices:

Harmondsworth, Middlesex, England

First published in 1991 by Viking Penguin,

a division of Penguin Books USA Inc.

10 9 8 7 6 5 4 3 2 1

Photograph credits appear on page 291.

Grateful acknowledgment is made for permission to reprint an excerpt from
"Plant a Radish" by Tom Jones and Harvey Schmidt. © 1963 Tom Jones, Harvey
Schmidt & Chappell & Co. Inc. All rights administered by Chappell & Co. Inc.
All rights reserved. Used by permission.

Library of Congress Cataloging-in-Publication Data

Chappellet, Molly.

    A vinyard garden / Molly Chappellet; foreword by Hugh Johnson;

  paintings by Lygia Chappellet; design by Jacqueline Jones Design.

       p.   cm.

  ISBN 0-670-83436-X

   1. Chappellet Vineyards Gardens (Saint Helena, Calif.).

 2. Chappellet Vineyards.   I. Title.

SB466.U7C483   1991

712' .6' 0979419—dc20   91-50165

Printed in Singapore

For Donn, with love

A Footpath Through
A Vineyard Garden

My first visit to the Chappellets' long low ranch-house high on Pritchard Hill remains vividly in my memory even twenty years later. California—the Napa Valley especially—is not short of great vistas, hillsides of great beauty, or perfectly sited homes and barns. But the long, expectant drive up Pritchard Hill, weaving among the madrone and live oak and buckeye, glimpsing shy deer among the rocks and unflinching red-tail hawks in the pine-tops, now catching sight of the green waters of Lake Hennessy far below, now confronted by the stiff battalions of vines, seemed at the time to encapsulate and to transcend them all. The drive climbs and curves and dips and climbs again, one moment in deep shade, the next in burning sun. Eventually it leaves behind the pastoral beauty of the valley farms to enter the rarer air of mountain meadows, where range answers purple range far up and down the coast. The cone of Mount Saint Helena rises to the north, its summit seemingly at eye level, the humble valleys between filling with evening light. It is not for the fainthearted, this landscape. To live in it is to confront heroic nature. Pritchard Hill challenges your concept of scale. This, as I read it, is the mainspring of Molly Chappellet's vision. She is an artist whose eyes have been opened wider than yours and mine by the sheer majesty and wonder of the eyrie where she and her family look out over the world. Donn Chappellet built a winery. That was the beginning of it. In the middle sixties, when nobody had built a new winery in the Napa Valley for thirty years, Robert Mondavi opened his famous mission-style winery down in Oakville. At the same time Donn and Molly Chappellet, refugees from Los Angeles with no wine-making antecedents, discovered a dramatic amphitheatre of vineyard perched high on Pritchard Hill. No conventional or nostalgic building would do for such a site. Instead they created a rust-coloured pyramid at its foot that still today, a quarter of a century later, remains the most radically modern, yet the most appropriate and harmonious, Napa winery of all. If I first climbed Pritchard Hill to visit a winery and taste early wines (which I still remember for their authority: they were firm, confident, even austere, dry Riesling and Chenin Blanc, and Cabernet as tannic as Latour),

I stayed, and kept on coming back, for the total experience of being with a truly creative family in full cry. I won't pretend the maturing wines did not constitute an ever-growing attraction: today they are among California's very finest, and singularly tuned for longevity, so that the pleasure of revisiting much-loved vintages is perpetually tempting. You could start with the rambling redwood house, bleached gray where it could be seen at all behind its ramps and bastions of spurge and azure echium, or dazzle-camouflaged by sunlight filtered through filigree maple leaves. The hilltop air seems to wash through its spaces: open easy rooms where brilliant colours have had time to mellow. Or you could start with Molly's vegetable garden: an almost surreal *potager* in fauve purples and grays and scarlet and soft blue out on the open hillside. Everywhere you turned you would find the sort of visual logic that leads to bold ideas without apology. A fallen bough would lie ignored on another hillside: Molly would see it as sculpture and install it—unselfconsciously with no hint of symbolism—on the white wall above the hearth. At Hallowe'en the terrace would erupt into a bazaar of pumpkins and gourds of unimagined shapes, sizes and colours. Everywhere there is evidence of a pair of eyes that take nothing for granted: a gift that can have the wonderful effect of making us ordinary purblind folk suddenly start seeing clearly too. A feeling of theatre comes into it. Anyone who sees the Chappellet winery decorated for a wine-tasting comes away with an image of Cabernets (once it was Romanée-Contis) as actors on a perfectly-lit, deftly-decorated stage. No wonder all San Francisco began to clamour for the Chappellet touch. Somehow, with the same economy of means married to lavishness of purpose, Molly took on whole ballrooms and transformed them into pageants of the seasons. Her technical mastery has increased—but her eye, her sensitivity to the visual moment, stays in the same diamond focus. This book is partly a record of some of her full-dress achievements. It can be used, if you like, as an advanced primer to study or emulate. Most of all, though, it is a book about seeing. It could open your eyes in the way that Walt Whitman opened your mind.

—*Hugh Johnson*

NATURE, WHETHER WILD OR CULTIVATED,
ALWAYS HAS BEEN AND
ALWAYS WILL BE THE BEST MODEL FOR
A WORTHWHILE EXISTENCE.
—PAUL HAWKEN

Twenty-something years ago our family moved from Beverly Hills to Pritchard Hill. There were seven of us—Donn, me, five children, and one on the way. Donn dreamed of making great wine, and I was willing to share that dream. We also shared a conviction that there was a simpler, more down-to-earth way to raise our family—and that we might find our own way in a more rural setting. Although we left Los Angeles, one of the world's busiest, liveliest cities, behind, life here on Pritchard Hill has been anything but uneventful. The early reputation of our wines brought many interesting guests to our door—and to our table. Hardly a day passed when Donn did not call from the winery and say, "Guess who's coming to dinner?" James Beard, Hugh Johnson, Danny Kaye, Laurence Harvey, Roger Vergé, Jean Troisgros, Dinah Shore, Clint Eastwood, Elizabeth David, Jeremiah Tower, Craig Claiborne, and on and on. Cooking, and gardening to supply ingredients, became a large part of our lives. The way things looked was as important to me as the way they tasted. With little help available, shortcuts were necessary, so I needed quick and simple solutions to bring beauty as well as nourishment to the table. Like most homemakers, I was, of course, juggling multiple hats—mother, chauffeur, cook, gardener, housekeeper, organizer, entertainer, and partial breadwinner. Wearing all those hats has been challenging and exhausting and exhilarating. Making the place we live, the food we eat, and the tables where we gather beautiful adds a vital and necessary ingredient to my life. A country environment has made me realize how essential it is in this age of computerized mechanization to reestablish our connection with the earth and bring back some part of that harmony and rhythm into our lives. And so the book is about just that. It's about the earth and things growing, and about enjoying them at each stage. It's celebrating ordinary occurrences, like sunlight filtering through leaf lettuce, or artichokes changing from vegetable to flower, or the brilliant green of moss after the rain. It's about adding beauty, whimsy, and drama to your everyday life. And so you'll find a few recipes for food included in this book, but there are also recipes for planting, parenting, composting, and arranging flowers, in the hope of nourishing in other ways than food. I hope you'll see that enjoyment of life does not come from learned skills but from curious eyes and an open heart.

THE WILD GARDEN

When we moved to Pritchard Hill, we discovered an unexpected bonus in the profusion of woods, rocks, and fields. At first I thought of these elements as "The Wilds," but soon I came to realize this was truly our *garden*, our wild garden. "Wild" and "garden" hardly seem to go together in the same sentence, never mind the same phrase. "The Wilds" conjures up images of untamed space—free, borderless, untouched by the hand of man—while "garden" implies man-made order, a plot of land organized, cared for, and controlled. There are, in fact, great similarities between "the wilds" and "the garden." Both are in a state of constant growth and change. That means that whatever the garden—wild or cultivated—there's always something different to see. Both gardens also require the same elements for survival—air, light, space, water, earth, warmth. Most important, both provide a place of refuge; a quiet place to play, rest, and contemplate. What sets gardens apart, one from the other, is human intervention. It doesn't matter that we didn't invent, choose, or plant the seeds, rocks, or trees. All these elements are here, gracious gifts to our planet millions of years ago. Without them, life as we know it wouldn't exist. And the earth keeps giving, whether in the wilds or in our cultivated gardens. We, and other creatures, are important, too. How else can the wild garden be appreciated?

The relationship of all living things is seen most clearly in the wilds. Is it mere coincidence that man has the same requirements—air, light, space, water, earth, and warmth—as nature? Is this why we find qualities in nature such as harshness and calmness, anticipation and sleepiness, gentleness and excitement, that we normally think of as human qualities? The surrounding hills, the lake below, the wooded acreage all around are still my favorite parts of the property. In them, and through them, I'm constantly inspired, instructed, and rejuvenated. Bringing back "found" treasures from nature is enriching. Introducing these "wild" elements into our cultivated garden and our home helps provide the stability and serenity otherwise missing from what seems like the breakneck pace of everyday life. Seeing these treasures recaptures the stillness—the sense of wonder, order, and harmony—that even a few moments alone in the wild garden afford. And that stillness nurtures me, renews me, and reassures me of our connection with the earth. Few days pass that I don't emerge from some wild, overgrown place, encrusted with heavy mud from field boots to fingertips, carrying an armful of these treasures. The uninitiated sometimes mistake these for just so many weeds, dead branches, leaves, moss, and seedpods. But I know better.

THE BOULDERS

And this our life, exempt

from public haunt,

Finds tongues in trees, books in

the running brooks,

Sermons in stones, and good

in every thing.

As You Like It

The first time I came to Pritchard Hill, I saw two things: a view that took my breath away and a small ranch house that nearly took my courage away.

When I arrived for my first official look at our home-to-be, Donn met me at the airport, and as we wended our way up the hill in his jeep—all the way, all the way—he "explained" to me that this property wasn't perfect—yet. But it would be a great place to grow the grapes we wanted to grow, grapes that would turn sweet and flavorful in dry, rough, rocky soil. And, he added, almost as an afterthought, what a view!

He was right. Seventeen hundred feet above the Napa Valley, we stood looking over lush, vine-covered slopes and the watery teal table of Lake Hennessy.

The view was breathtaking; the house was not— a low, graceless ranch-style building we—Donn, I, and all the children—would call home. It looked like a roughly executed false front for a low-budget Western, miraculously transplanted from the back lot at MGM up to Pritchard Hill. To add the coup de grace, it was painted motel-pink.

What I didn't see was that, long before we had come calling, long before any human creatures had made their way to Pritchard Hill, nature had studded the landscape with rocks so big and so heavy they could only be called "The Boulders."

EARLY DAYS ON PRITCHARD HILL

When we first bought the vineyard, we were mystified by the planting pattern—a few rows of grapevines, interspersed at haphazard intervals with large overgrown patches, wild with weeds. As we began cultivating, however, the reason for this configuration became clear. Everywhere the land looked wild, there were rocks—islands of boulders, many the size of dinosaurs. But what's a rock or two or three thousand to a family bent on bringing efficiency to the land? The boulder islands would have to go.

Six weeks and several thousand dollars later, we had invaded Pritchard Hill with monster-size D8 bulldozers, several kegs of dynamite, and plenty of familial sweat. We had only partial success—five of the twenty rocky mounds had been vanquished. But then we were faced with another, more immediate problem: what to do with the masses of rock we had harvested. All at once, we understood why the Napa Valley was replete with stone structures—barns, wineries, homes, commercial buildings. Stone was the building material Mother Nature supplied in abundance.

WORKING ON THE STONE GANG

I had always loved the look and the substance of stone buildings, from the ruined wineries and abbeys of Europe to the storybook churches of New England. So I was excited about the prospect of creating our own stone winery. But not for long. The modern building codes, to our dismay, made the use of stone as construction material virtually impossible.

Still, the rocks remained. So we organized our teenage sons in a kind of "volunteer" chain gang. They set to picking rocks, filling truckloads to be hauled away, and helping us stockpile them for future use. They were less than happy laborers, but as I filled them with meals and watched them turn brown and flex their developing biceps, I thought: There are worse ways for teenage boys to spend a summer.

Meanwhile, the boulders and I were developing a very personal—and frustrating—relationship. "Motel 6," as the kids affectionately called our rambling farmhouse, was shaded by almost nothing on one side. When the hot Napa sun beat in, if it were 110 degrees outside, it would be 115 degrees inside. So I began planting for shade.

But invariably, anywhere, everywhere I wanted to plant a tree, or a shrub, or a vine, there was a boulder.

Heavy boulders were chiseled into slabs to build the mantel of this fireplace in our neighbor's home. The massive chimney was formed with fieldstone selected for size and color from the vineyard. Grouped under a madrone branch, small moss-encrusted rocks add to the woodland imagery.

My collection of broken grape stakes, shovels, and picks grew. Donn would remind me, every time I exploded in frustration, that the best grapes grow in rocky, gravelly soil. Mm-hmm. My vision of symmetric, straight vineyard rows, surrounded by acres of green hills, with manicured gardens of flowers, herbs, and vegetables, was retreating into a fantasy.

But the beauty and the power of the boulders had started to seduce me. When another hoe handle broke, I would remind my helpers—and myself—that stones helped shape the people we are. There were the cave paintings at Lascaux, there were man's first tools and weapons, there was, I said, warming to my lecture, that wonderful word "troglodyte," a much more appealing locution than "cave dweller."

As the rocks reappeared each year in the vineyard, I kept questioning their origin. Mount St. Helena (clearly visible from our property), with its flat top, was said to have been an active volcano a few thousand years ago and was responsible for our stones. Later we heard that it was Mount Konocti, some fifty miles away, that had erupted and produced our volcanic rock.

Last year, when drilling a well, a geologist finally set us straight. Two separate geologic "units" underlie this area, the Sonoma Volcanics and the Great Valley Formation. The Sonoma Volcanics is a group of lava flows and beds of volcanic ash that were laid down on an

13

old land surface several million years ago. Underlying
the Volcanics is the marine sediment of the eighty-to-
one-hundred-million-year-old Great Valley Formation,
with a thickness of several thousand feet.

While the geology is interesting, it's the sheer
beauty of stone that is the most compelling to me.
Elegant veined marble, flagstone, and rich slates—what
man-made building materials could rival these for
splendor and durability?

Oh, yes, I could muster quite a pretty sermon
from the stones.

But my draftee assistants remained unmoved, as
did the boulders.

We talk about people—and relationships—being
solid as a rock. There is no better description of solidity
and dependability. I would think about this after finding
one favorite boulder, conveniently flattened on one side
for a seat, warmed by the sun, and ready for me to take a
rest. I would look out over the hill, and think about the
fact that long before we came, the rocks were here, and
long after we leave, they will still be here on Pritchard
Hill. Others will muscle them around—or learn to live
with them. Some will find the perfect seat or picnic table.
We are mutable; the boulders are not.

*O*riginally part of the
Sonoma Volcanics,
these giant-scale boulders
were deposited on
Pritchard Hill by a lava
flow millions of years ago.
Unearthed during the
clearing of the vineyard,
today they determine
the rhythm of the
landscape. Indoors, small
boulders provide function
and form. This one
supports William
Thackeray and Victor
Hugo.

FINDING OUR MARK

One day, however, something happened to change forever our outlook on the rock quarry we called home.

In Los Angeles, we had lived lawn by lawn, house by house, for years without a single argument from neighbors about boundaries, borders, or walls. But here in the country, surrounded by open acres and acres of land, we suddenly found ourselves in a dispute with a neighbor over property lines. We retained a licensed surveyor, and Donn set out over the property, 1869 hand-written survey map in hand, with two vineyard men along, wielding machetes to help clear the way. Out they went, looking for markers. The survey note indicated that many marks had been made on trees, singly or in groups. Lightning, storms, and the years had erased most of these signs. But then we found the crucial insignia that would settle the dispute—a figure 8 on a huge boulder, unscathed by a century of weather. Both Donn and I gained new respect for the boulders and the permanence they gave our claim.

It is symbolic of the peace we made with our boulders that when we dedicated our new winery, we let the children place their handprints in a bit of cement, except for the youngest, Dominic. We pressed his tiny, three-inch foot into the gloppy mess instead. We wanted a rock-like, permanent record of the day, of the place, and of our joy in being there.

PRITCHARD HILL POT PIE

Supper in the Old Stone Wine Cellar is Donn's favorite meal for a number of reasons. He loves all the different flavors that keep appearing, flavors that complement his cabernet. He loves flaky piecrusts, and he likes the fact that pot pies stay hot, which forces everyone to eat slowly and enjoy the wine. Since this is a rather time-consuming recipe, I make my pie dough a day ahead, roll out, cut into rounds, layer with waxed paper, and store in refrigerator. I also trim and cut the meats— and even cook them—a day ahead.

Enough pastry dough for 3 double-crust 9-inch pies
1½ pounds each boneless lean beef and lamb, trimmed of fat, cut into 1-inch cubes, and dredged in flour
½ pound Polish sausages
2 tablespoons rendered bacon fat (optional)
1 cup cabernet sauvignon
2 small onions, each stuck with 1 whole clove
2 medium carrots, cut into chunks
1 bay leaf, halved
3 sprigs each thyme and parsley
1 sprig rosemary
1 celery stalk, cut in half, for bouquet garni
2 cups each rich veal stock and rich chicken stock
2 teaspoons glace de viande
(can be purchased in specialty shops as meat glaze or meat extract)
Salt and freshly ground black pepper to taste
2 teaspoons cinnamon
30 very small carrots, blanched 5 minutes
30 pearl onions, blanched 5 minutes
4 turnips, blanched 5 minutes and then cut into bite-size pieces
3 celery stalks, sliced ⅜ inch thick
½ cup cognac
1 tablespoon butter
½ pound fresh mushrooms (wild, if available), cut into bite-size pieces
3 shallots, chopped
2 cloves garlic, chopped
1 red bell pepper, seeded and coarsely chopped
4 medium zucchini, cut into bite-size pieces
5 kumquats, thinly sliced and seeded, or 2 tablespoons lemon zest
½ cup chopped parsley

Make the pastry dough and set aside in the refrigerator.

In a large skillet, begin sautéing beef and sausages together. If sausage fat does not provide sufficient liquid, add up to 2 tablespoons bacon fat. Remove beef and sausages from pan when browned and transfer the beef to a large saucepan. Let sausages cool, skin, slice 1 inch thick, and set aside. In the same pan in which beef was sautéed, sauté lamb. After lamb is browned, transfer to a separate plate. Deglaze skillet with cabernet sauvignon and add scrapings to the pan containing the beef. Cover beef with water and add the 2 onions and 2 carrots. Make bouquet garni by placing the bay leaf, thyme, parsley, and rosemary in the hollow of the celery stalks, tying the stalks with string. Add the bouquet garni to the

beef and bring to a boil, then turn heat down and simmer for an hour. Add the cooked lamb and enough water to cover. Cook until lamb is tender, about 45 minutes.

With a slotted spoon, transfer meats to a giant stockpot. Strain the cooking liquid, discarding herbs and vegetables. Boil liquid until it is reduced to 1½ quarts; then pour over the meats in the stockpot. Add reserved sausage, veal stock, chicken stock, and glace de viande. Season with salt and pepper and add the cinnamon.

Bring mixture to a boil, add small carrots, pearl onions, turnips, celery, and cognac and simmer 10–15 minutes.

In a skillet, melt the butter, add the mushrooms, shallots, and garlic, and sauté until garlic is transparent. Add the

bell pepper. Cook 3 to 4 minutes. Add mushroom mixture to meats along with raw zucchini.

Spoon an equal portion of the meat-and-vegetable mixture into each of ten individual baking dishes, each with a capacity of about 1½ cups. Add a few kumquat slices or some lemon zest to each dish and sprinkle each with a spoonful of parsley.

Roll out pastry dough and cut into rounds 1 inch larger than baking dishes. Top each dish with a pastry round, pressing edges firmly against the rim of the dish and fluting them. Prick with fork. Bake pies in a preheated 425-degree oven for 15 minutes, or until crusts are golden brown and pies are heated through.

Serves 10

MAKING PEACE WITH THE STONES

The children came to peace with the stones in an entirely different way. When they weren't picking or hauling, it seemed, they looked upon those same infernal rocks as the perfect playground. Who needed a jungle gym when there were rocks? The children would clamber up and down on them, play King of the Mountain on them, and, as kamikaze pilots, take death-defying flying leaps from their heights.

The toddlers liked the smaller stones, too, the river-washed rocks that we used to pave the driveway. They thought the pea-sized gravel so interesting in shape and color that it must be edible. When they discovered it wasn't, they stowed the little pebbles away in pockets as a surprise for the washing machine.

Although raking the three-hundred-foot driveway was the boys' weekly chore, they preferred to make their marks in the gravel on their bicycles, executing sharp turns in a shower of stones. Repeatedly, I tried to describe for them the meditative state that can be reached through the sound of the large metal rake dragging across the sea of gravel. Somehow, although they did their chore, they never seemed to share my sense of serenity and satisfaction that came with making quiet order and beauty in our driveway entrance.

This rock with a hollow in the middle is perfect for washing the dirt from root vegetables or to leave filled with water for a birdbath.

Lynn, Sequoia, and Luke Amaru climb on nature's jungle gym.

In the Arden forest, Shakespeare found
sermons in stones. On Pritchard Hill, we found
pathways. Carissa, our middle daughter, discovered
a natural outcropping of flagstone in a cluster of
boulders. An eighteen-year-old friend, with impressive
muscles developed from competitive javelin throwing,
conned our nine- and ten-year-old boys into a work
force. For weeks they excavated and relocated yards of
flagstone into pathways around our home.

Our oldest daughter, Lygia, and two high-
energy friends were determined to match the boys'
efforts. They devoted part of their summer to clearing
a rock quarry and constructing the first retaining
wall there for our new vegetable garden. Much was
percolating in Lygia's young head, as she and her
girlfriends giggled and sweated over those stones. As an
adult, she has drawn inspiration from the boulders for
her paintings. Today, bold lines and subtle gradations of
earthy colors adorn Lygia's silks and canvases, recalling
the power and majesty of the rocks she used to haul.

THE GEOGRAPHY OF ROCKS

The boulders of Pritchard
Hill heighten my awareness of rocks wherever I go. I
love the punctuation they give to a landscape, the sense
of drama and permanence, and the strong sense of
character each kind of rock adds to its home.

*The drone of
working bees is the only
sound heard as
the cherry blossoms fall
silently to the ground.
Petals are deliberately left
where the gentle
winds have pushed them,
making a beautiful
pattern between the
stones.*

BREAKFAST ON A BOULDER:
ALEXA'S SEEDS AND SUCH BREAD

Lygia makes a great herb bread, Cyril a rosemary and olive bread, Jon-Mark a jalapeño brioche. and Donn has now entered the scene with his electric bread machine. But Alexa's bread is a rich, moist, healthful, satisfying meal in itself.

¾ cup wheat berries

⅛ cup rye berries

⅛ cup buckwheat groats

3 ½ cups warm water

2 packages active dry yeast

1 teaspoon honey

½ cup molasses

1 tablespoon salt

¼ cup melted butter

3 cups rye flour

3 cups wheat flour

2 cups white flour

⅓ cup bran

½ cup sunflower seeds

¼ cup sesame seeds

2 tablespoons poppy seeds

Soak whole grains overnight or cook until almost soft.

Place 3 ½ cups warm water in a large bowl. Add yeast and honey and stir to dissolve. Let stand about 5 minutes, or until foamy.

Combine molasses, salt, and melted butter in the bowl of an electric mixer fitted with a dough hook. Add yeast mixture and combine thoroughly.

At low speed, add flours and bran—one at a time. Add the drained grains, then mix in the seeds. Keep mixer on low speed for 5 to 7 minutes.

Move bowl to a warm area, cover, and let dough rise for about 1 ½ to 2 hours.

Punch down dough (you may need a bit more flour if it is sticky), divide in two and shape into loaves. Place each in a lightly buttered standard-size loaf pan.

Bake in a preheated 350-degree oven for about 45 minutes (or up to 1 hour) or until brown and loaves sound hollow when tapped. Turn out on racks to cool.

Yield: 2 loaves

JAMMING WITH CYRIL

Two things make Cyril's jams unusual. He often cooks two or three fruits together as a base syrup, which adds complexity of flavor as well as color; and he barely cooks his whole, unpeeled fruit, which allows the fresh fruit flavor to come through.

Cyril's method for jamming is something like this.

Jars are placed in a pan of water and sterilized in an oven at 400 degrees while he's cooking his base syrup. Base syrup might be sugar with strawberries, pitted cherries, or plums. He cooks down the syrup and adds a little pectin.

When the syrup has thickened, he adds his main fruit for jam—such as peaches. The syrup is brought back to a full boil and removed from the heat.

Then he lifts fruit gently from the pot and fills jars, adding syrup to ¼ inch from top. He tightens the lids firmly and lets the jars cool.

I love the warm colors and jagged drama of the Arizona cliffs, shapes that take your breath away as you wind from Phoenix up into the cooler air of Flagstaff.

Another favorite is the blue and flinty shapes of the New England coast, visible reminders of the kind of people who courageously carved a new life out of what must have seemed an alien and inhospitable shore.

South of Pritchard Hill, south of California entirely, there are the sand-colored boulders studding the Sea of Cortez. These are rocks on a grand scale, their shapes jutting into silhouettes against the wide and starry sky and blue-green sea. There are the chalky cliffs of Dover and the stark and rugged craters of southern Italy and Greece. There is a boulder-lover's world tour waiting to happen, I just know.

For me, it is the drama and majesty of the rocks that lure me. Thirteen of them signal visitors that they have arrived at our home and our winery. I like to think of them as elegant opening statements, communicating the stateliness you get from the warm, opening notes of Mussorgsky's *Pictures at an Exhibition*, or the excitement of the brassy first measures in Tchaikovsky's Fourth.

Smooth river stones make wonderfully touchable paperweights.

Large lichen-covered rocks, when seen in a new environment, are easily recognized as sculpture.

WOOING THE EARTH

My friends tease me because it seems as if the rocks have taken up residence, not just outside, as you would expect, but inside as well. Heated in the oven, they're perfect warmers for a breadbasket; they hold doors open, weight my flower and vegetable arrangements, and keep a cookbook open while I peer at a recipe next to the stove.

Which brings me back to the reason we came here, looking for a rocky place to start a vineyard. Our grapes struggle to put down roots in the stony soil, but, as Donn predicted, they become more remarkable for the struggle. Heartland gardeners know that parsnips really do grow sweeter in the snow. We don't generally have snow in the Napa Valley, but we have rocks for hardship—and for pleasure—and we are better farmers, vintners, and people for the gifts they give us.

When I see the ways we and the rocks live together every day, I understand what the Bengali poet Rabindranath Tagore meant about "wooing the earth." In fact, the earth has wooed us—and we will be friends and lovers for life.

THE WOODS

*The woods are
made for the hunters
of dreams.*

SAM WALTER FOSS

Whenever I enter the woods, whatever the season or time of day, something magical happens. I experience another dimension, moving from the garden or the boulders into the woods. It's a little like stepping from an open beach into the sea; the air I breathe and the sensation I feel underfoot is suddenly—different.

My heart slows down. All of my senses grow quiet, yet more alive, somehow more open to the mysteries and pleasures the woods have to offer. If someone is with me, we find ourselves whispering so as not to disturb the silence.

Woods are truly enchanted places, where strange and fanciful things take place. In children's stories, they are populated with nymphs, fairies, sprites, perhaps a druid or two thrown in for good measure. There is, of course, a certain duality in the woods: there, Hansel and Gretel encountered and vanquished the witch, Little Red Riding Hood met up with the wolf, and Daphne was turned into a laurel tree to protect her from Apollo's advances. Our woods have always seemed warm and friendly to me, a likely setting for magic—not trouble. As Stephen Sondheim correctly perceived, all sorts of mystical and wonderful things can happen when we go *Into the Woods*.

The *visual* is the feast to which I'm most naturally drawn. I experience things by seeing them, by observing. But when musicians visit, they remind me to be aware of the aural splendors as well. There is a symphony in our woods. Sometimes it's just the air, stirring the trees, each branch finding its own tune with its leaves or needles. Sometimes it's the birds and insects, twittering, chattering, calling out to each other. Sometimes the tones are lower-pitched. Mountain lions, deer, and raccoon make their homes here. Wild boars roam in drifts, disturbing the earth like natural Rototillers, sharing space with moles, voles, skunks, and squirrels.

THE MUSIC OF THE WOODS

No wonder composers have found inspiration in the natural sounds of the woods. I think of the plaintive theme of Debussy's *Afternoon of a Faun*, Franz Lehár's frothy *Where the Lark Sings*, Strauss's lyric *Tales from the Vienna Woods*, and the rustic folk motifs from Smetana's music. Flutes and woodwinds seem the instruments that best give voice to the sound and character of the woods. I always think of *Peter and the Wolf* and Peter's playful oboe theme as "forester's music."

One exception to this woodland medley proved
most memorable—a walk I took through another forest,
in the Sierras, right after a snowstorm. Even now, ten
years later, my strongest impression of that solitary walk
was the incredible stillness around me. I remember the
deep hush that new-fallen snow brings to everything,
even human footsteps. The tall, straight pines,
surrounding me like silent sentinels, seemed to savor the
quiet as much as I.

PLEASURES UNDERFOOT

On an ordinary, non-
snowy day, my footsteps make sounds out in the woods.
And those sounds remind me to look down. There are
such wonders underfoot. Often I see what's at my feet as
an amazing mosaic of fallen leaves and bark, sticks,
acorns, mosses, and pods. The best time to appreciate
this woodland litter is after a winter rain. Then the
colors range from copper to mahogany, from palest
terra-cotta to rich, dark brown. In autumn, the palette is
lighter—yellows, amber, gold, rust, burgundy. It's not
enough for me to take the memory of those rich colors,
textures, and aromas back home. I carry a basket with
me on autumn walks to collect this artistic mulch and
turn it into a woodland potpourri. In a large old copper
bowl or earthenware dish, the rich scent evokes forays
into the forest for weeks to come.

Donn's favorite harvest from the forest floor is culinary. On warm days after a rain in fall or early spring, delicate fungi appear. His eyes are sharp enough to spot a golden chanterelle hiding under a blanket of leaves. When he's been successful on his quest, we know there will be a special feast that night.

The woods are the perfect place to remember that we don't just see with our eyes; we can look with our feet as well. Just the feel of the forest floor can tell you what season it is—damp and slippery in the winter, light and spongy in the spring, dry and firm in the summer, and crisp and crackly in the fall.

THE FOUR SEASONS

In the summertime, the woods are a welcome and cool haven. The green leaves provide a natural canopy and shelter from the heat. In autumn, there's such a tapestry of color and sound, all those leaves changing hue, all those drying twigs and dried leaves rustling underfoot. The forest floor has taught me, as a gardener, to respect that carpet of leaves as mulch-in-the-making. Every year, trees become eminently practical, casting aside their raiment, carelessly littering the ground with fallen leaves. A mature oak sheds about two hundred fifty thousand leaves every fall.

When woodland potpourri has properly aged, it is refreshing, slightly spicy, and, of course, woodsy. Small cones and pine needles are combined with bark and leaves of madrone, manzanita, oak, and bay (recipe, page 54).

Making pine needle baskets, a craft we've learned from the Native Americans, is a very slow, tedious process. After five hours of concentration and agile finger coordination, I was able to make something resembling a coaster. My sister-in-law Claire, far more patient than I, made these magnificent baskets.

Pine needle baskets are extremely strong and will last more than one lifetime, handed down from one generation to the next. The intense smell of pine lingers almost as long as the baskets survive.

You will need a large supply of long, three-pronged pine needles; a long, dull sewing needle; twine; reeds; and grass or raffia. An infinite amount of patience, nimble fingers, and hand-eye coordination are critical components of the craft.

Enjoy a walk collecting needles (this is the best part!). Spread the needles out to dry until they are light green in color. When ready to begin weaving, plunge a small bundle of needles in water to keep them pliable while using. Grouping the needles in twos or threes and holding them in place while you braid or tie raffia is the difficult part. There are several stitches that can be used. The one we've used here is a little like the crochet chain stitch.

On Pritchard Hill, we aim for that same practicality. Everything organic that we discard—leaves, cut flowers, food wastes—goes back into the earth to decompose and nourish the next generation of growing things.

But to me, winter and early spring are the most provocative seasons in the woods. In the winter, I see trees in a brand-new way, stripped to their essential sculptured forms and shapes. And, though many leaves are gone, there are newer, fresher greens to see. Velvet, bottle-green moss covers boulders and tree trunks after the first rain. Then there's lichen, that strange symbiosis of fungus and algae. The fungus contributes a host, water, and minerals, and the algae bring food to the party, food produced by photosynthesis. It would seem that lichens are not choosy; there are more than fifteen thousand species, occurring in most terrestrial habitats from the Arctic and Antarctic to the tropics. But lichen is selective—it will not grow in polluted air.

So, there they are, moss and lichen, Cinderella's drab stepsisters most of the year, faded and brown. Moisture is the fairy godmother that transforms them overnight to brilliant gold or emerald green. Not just splendid for the looking, either, but irresistible to the touch as well.

The various shades and textures of lichen and moss have continued to inspire me. I was so enchanted by the brilliant contrast of the lichens—chartreuses against a calm gray-green—that I designed an entrance using that color scheme. Adding a bluish-green wash to a drab brown fence created a perfect background, one

that set off a bright chartreuse front door. The colors that surprise and delight in nature add the same enchantment to a front entryway.

THINKING SMALL:
SEQUOIA AND THE GARDEN

I've had a few companions on winter walks in the woods, but none I cherish as much as my five-year-old granddaughter, Sequoia. She is well named, this little girl with a *sempervirens* imagination. She is at home in the woods, and, as if by magic, the forest opens secrets to her I might never see.

One January morning, Sequoia and I were clomping along in our field boots, holding hands, looking for mushrooms. I confess to being a little distracted, struggling for some fresh ideas to bring to a seminar I was scheduled to lead at Macy's department store. Sequoia had the answer. Though we started out looking for mushrooms, soon she began cooking up sumptuous miniature moss gardens. Following her lead, I carefully lifted clumps of moss so that they could later be returned to their habitats. The seedpods we placed on top of the moss miraculously became mini-boulders; tiny, leafed branches we arranged at intervals became trees. Irish moss created a field of tiny white buds.

In Sequoia's mini-moss garden, moss, lichen, fern, and miner's lettuce from the wild garden are interspersed with chrysanthemums, forget-me-nots, santolina, feverfew, and lamb's ears from the cultivated garden.

Sequoia's fantasy garden became the star of my seminar, and I was able to report that the only tools required to assemble these dwarf landscapes were a big kitchen spoon, a spatula, a basket, a spray bottle, and a child's unfettered imagination—along with a forest, of course.

WINTER SECRETS

Winter nudity exposes a tree's secrets. The bark of a tree is not unlike our own skin, protecting the interior and keeping a vivid, indelible history of traumas that may have been endured. The careful observer of a tree can see where last year's branches grew, or where they were thwarted. You can tell if the tree went thirsty, stressed for lack of water, or if it grew rapidly. And, just like us, as a tree gets older its "wrinkles" grow deeper. The texture of new branches on most trees is smooth and often lighter in color than on older trees. If you've ever touched new young limbs on a California laurel, you know what a sensual pleasure the smooth, fawn-colored bark gives back.

Tree bark protects us as well as the tree. Both eucalyptus and redwood barks are fire-resistant; if only they could guarantee that the forests would remain safe from fire.

Occasionally, I wonder how many of our grand oaks on Pritchard Hill are the living legacies of absentminded squirrels. Years ago, on the road back from the winery, we found a baby tree squirrel, hopelessly circling its dead mother. Donn gently lifted the tiny animal, put it in his shirt pocket, drove home, and began nursing it with an eyedropper. For six months we shared our bathroom with the tiny creature. He grew busy as he grew bigger, burying nuts and acorns in the bathroom carpet. He rarely returned to retrieve them. Since the bathroom carpet wasn't organic, none of his buried treasure ever grew up to be oak trees. But, ah, if they had been buried out of doors, what a forest we might have!

When I think about that squirrel and his apparently haphazard planting, I think of a more deliberate approach to growing forests. I think of Elzéard Bouffier, a French shepherd and wanderer who, during the last thirty-seven years of his life, planted a hundred acorns every day in the wilderness. Some sprouted, some did not. Of those that sprouted, some fell victim to animals or natural disaster. But those that remained grew into seedlings, and then into trees, trees that would not have been there without Bouffier's efforts. When he died in 1947, his oak trees had completely changed the ecology of a previously desolate

Although a tree heals itself when it loses a limb, the scar remains. The swirling circular pattern of the knot is visible in every form the tree takes, whether a wall panel, a bowl, or a table.

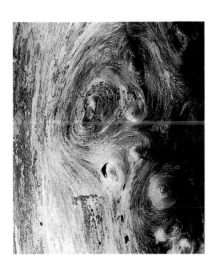

WOODLAND POTPOURRI

Potpourri from the woods can be made any time of the year, but the early fall, after a gentle rain has washed off the summer dust, is the ideal time for colorful leaves and seedpods to be scattered on the ground. I like woodland potpourri to be quite bold both in texture and in fragrance. Keeping the pieces large seems to suit the woodsy theme. All materials must be completely dry.

> *4 cups assorted leaf litter*
> *2 cups bark and wood shavings*
> *3 cups green conifer needles, such as white fir and balsam,*
> *or other aromatic needles*
> *2 cups seeds, pods, nuts, and acorns*
> *2 handfuls small pinecones*
> *1 large container—a basket or a glass, crockery, or copper bowl*

Toss all the ingredients gently with your fingertips and enjoy the fragrance and earthy touch of the woods.

VARIATIONS

Substitute rosemary branches and dried sage for the conifer needles. Grind the rosemary and add three teaspoons orrisroot (a fixative that allows scents to release slowly) and a few drops of sandalwood oil.

For a spicier potpourri, especially nice at Christmastime, add eight ½-inch strips of orange peel, 3 teaspoons orrisroot, 4 drops sandalwood oil, 5 drops cinnamon oil, four 2-inch cinnamon sticks, and 3 whole cloves ground in a food processor.

Mix oils and powders together with your fingers, add to dry ingredients, and toss with your hands. Seal tightly in a closed container or put strong plastic wrap on top of the bowl. Let sit for about six weeks, turning the container upside down every few days.

Remembering that scents attract, excite, repel, or calm, I like to make recipes of woodland potpourri in various strengths. I put a strong, spicier scent in areas where we don't spend much time—closets and bathrooms. A more mellow mixture goes into the bedroom or living room.

The mahogany peelings of the manzanita and the two-tone curly bark of the madrone make colorful additions to our woodland potpourri.

landscape. He was, as writer Jean Giono described him in the title of his book, *The Man Who Planted Hope and Grew Happiness*. In some small way, we try to follow Bouffier's example on Pritchard Hill. We gather and plant acorns and transplant seedlings from the wilds—oaks, manzanitas, maples—and put them where they are needed and where we hope they will flourish.

APPRECIATING ARBUTUS AND ARCTOSTAPHYLOS

Here in our woods, the madrones *(Arbutus menziesii)* and manzanitas *(Arctostaphylos manzanita)* sport the most startling bark. Both are so smooth they appear polished, and shine with a reddish hue.

The madrones, a member of the heath family (which also includes rhododendrons and azaleas), offer one spectacular sight after another. In the spring, clusters of bell-shaped flowers, white to pinkish, appear. In the fall, clusters of bright red and orange-colored berries remind us of the madrone's cousin, the strawberry tree. The back sides of the leaves are a shimmery silver, and on a damp, cold night when lamplight or moonlight falls upon these trees, they look absolutely incandescent.

Of the fifty or so species of manzanita, forty-three are at home in California. I had never seen manzanita until I came to Northern California.

It is unmistakable, with its dark red bark and gray-green leaves. The entire bush turns into a million cream-colored dots in January, when it produces small shell-like blossoms with pinkish overtones.

Both manzanitas and madrones are like shedding snakes, constantly peeling their outer coverings to reveal the beauty underneath. In the manzanita, a magnificent mahogany lies just under the bark. A stunning copper and green lie under the madrone bark. I use the madrone bark peelings for dye in my weaving projects, trying to enjoy the rich, brownish-red color I love in nature in another medium.

One evening not long ago, while it was raining, I took a drive down our vineyard road past the woods with my three-year-old granddaughter, Luke Amaru. She sat quietly in the car, pressing her rosebud nose to the cool window, trying to sniff raindrops. Suddenly she was overcome with excitement. "Look! Look! Look!" she cried, pointing to a grove of rain-slick madrones, trunks glistening like copper sealskin, leaves lit up like silver fire in the headlights from the car. We had to stop so that Luke Amaru could jump out and see just how these exotic wooden sculptures felt. So we did—and she was right to demand the detour.

The colors of winter come as such a gift to us, spots of brightness when the rest of the world seems cold, gray, and dark. If you've ever wondered where the traditional colors of Christmas—red and green—come from, you have nature to thank. The dark greens of hollies and evergreens, the bright reds of berry

An autumn swag of dried silvery madrone leaves, coppery manzanita, ailanthus seed pods, and dried hydrangea blossoms welcome guests through the front door, made from recycled old wood. The door handle is a piece of driftwood from the Rouge River.

Straight, almost surreal limbs from California laurel are nailed to 6 x 1-inch boards, bringing the woods to our dining table.

ornaments—together they make us feel secure and warm in the cold of winter. They are a reminder, too, that new life is coming, that the earth is only dormant, waiting to be stirred by spring.

WINTER INDOORS

I love filling the house with winter greens. If you don't have trees of your own, the flower marts are full of a variety of raw materials. Nothing is prettier than a combination of evergreen leaves and needles. Add a little contrast with California laurel—aromatic, yellow-green, and long-lasting.

One of my most amusing winter bouquets was created the year everything froze in the Napa Valley. Usually our valley is renowned for its temperate climate. But this particular winter, we had five straight days of weather below twenty degrees. The old-timers shook their heads and assured us this happens only every half century or so. But that was little consolation to my blackened pelargonium, echium, artichokes, and, especially, citrus orchard.

But life goes on, even in the cold and dark. And, in fact, people feel more need than ever to gather together when it seems bleak outside. A friend planned a spur-of-the-moment potluck dinner and phoned with a challenging request: could I bring a bouquet for the entrance hall and to decorate her dining table?

Once this oak barrel—
the wood for which came
from the forests of
France, not unlike the
woods on Pritchard Hill—
was used to age and
impart flavor to our wine.
But no matter how
many different uses this
oak has during its lifetime,
it will eventually fill
another purpose: to
decompose and thereby
rejuvenate the earth.

CHANTERELLES AND
CHARDONNAY

Finding golden
chanterelles, which Donn
often does along the path
to the winery, is almost as
good as finding gold.
Colleen McGlinn's spaetzle
is a great unexpected
accompaniment to these
mushrooms. The
chanterelles are simply
sautéed in butter with
garlic, shallots, and thyme,
then served around a
mound of spaetzle drizzled
with olive oil and topped
with fried sage—perfect
with chardonnay.

I said yes in one moment and thought, "What a wicked trick!" in the next. There wasn't a flower in my garden, and at that late hour, both florist's shops were closed.

But I'd already said yes. . . . So I bundled up and headed straight for the woods. Things didn't seem quite so depressing there. (I averted my eyes from all the frost-blasted blooms as I walked through the garden.) It seemed right to see barren limbs overhead, and broken dead branches strewn across the forest floor. I collected about a dozen straight limbs, eight feet long, crusted with lichen and moss. I carried them to my friend's home, stood them in a deep, dark wooden bucket, and paced back to survey the effect. They looked quite regal and important enough for the lofty entrance hall.

As for the table, that was another matter. The ruined scene in my garden brought tears to my eyes, but, bravely, I gathered all the browned and blackened flowers I could find. I added some gray and copper leaves, twigs, and freeze-dried ferns to the collection, and created—well, something.

But it was perfect! My hostess howled when she saw this monochromatic bouquet, reminiscent as it was of her own garden. It wasn't the most gorgeous, the most sumptuous centerpiece, but it was one of the funniest. And, given the time and place, certainly natural.

Branches of the buckeye at every stage of development—horse chestnuts hanging on dormant branches or limbs in full bloom—are great to use indoors. Blossoms cut and brought inside before the buds open will last at least ten days, slowly releasing their fragrance and exhibiting their delicate pink interiors.

DONN'S VERSION OF DINAH SHORE'S BISCUITS

When Donn and our good friend Dinah Shore get together in the kitchen, great things happen. Both of them make unbeatable (in every way) biscuits. I think I overheard the secret—something about "light fingers, barely touch, leave lumpy." Donn, of course, can't resist the butter temptation, so he substitutes ¼ cup butter for ¼ cup of Dinah's shortening.

2 cups sifted flour
2 teaspoons baking powder
½ teaspoon salt
¼ cup butter
¼ cup shortening
1 cup plus 2 tablespoons buttermilk

Preheat oven to 400 degrees. Sift dry ingredients together into a medium mixing bowl. Using two knives, cut butter and shortening into dry ingredients until the mixture resembles coarse crumbs. Gradually add buttermilk, stirring gently until dough is sticky and not dry.

Turn dough out onto a floured board. Handling the dough as little as possible, pat it into a ½-inch-thick circle. Then cut with a 2-inch biscuit cutter. After you have cut out as many circles as you can, pinch the remaining dough together and make one last irregular biscuit for yourself. Place biscuits on a greased cookie sheet so that circles don't touch. Bake for 10 minutes, or until brown. Serve hot.

Yield: about 12 biscuits

WILD BLACKBERRY SANDWICHES

When the wild blackberries are really, really ripe—so dark they've changed from purple to near-black—we know it's time for wild blackberry sandwiches. All it takes is a batch of buttermilk biscuits, hot and just out of the oven, and a jar of cream. We wrap them well, put them in a basket with a flat rock heated in the oven while the biscuits baked, and head for the woods. We fill the basket with berries, slit the biscuits open, pour on a little cream, layer the berries between the biscuit halves, close them up so that the berries crush and send their juices into the biscuits—and then, mmmm.

IN NORTHERN CALIFORNIA IN JANUARY,
WHEN MANY TREES ARE DORMANT,
MANZANITA TREES ARE COVERED WITH
TINY BLOSSOMS, A WELCOME SIGHT.

THE OMNIPOTENT GODDESS

The American poet e. e. cummings called spring the "omnipotent goddess," and I believe he was right. Anticipating her return, after weeks and months of cold, rain, even snow, I like to bring some hint of spring indoors.

Here in the Napa Valley we seem to have one extra season. It comes around in February, when the sun appears, warm and wonderful, and suddenly we have almond blossoms, golden flowering mimosa, bright yellow mustard. Once again, we're tricked into thinking spring is here.

During this false spring the dormant buckeye trees *(Aesculus californica)*, relatives of the horse chestnut, begin to develop miniature green "candles" at the tip of each branch. I think of them as early signals, sent out to awaken the other deciduous trees still fast asleep in the forest. I love to cut a couple of buckeye limbs at this stage and bring them indoors, to watch firsthand the magic of spring.

Seeing them open is like watching a toddler take her first step. In the beginning, as the baby buckeye leaves unfurl, they stand stiffly erect, as if unsure of their new position. Then, after growing accustomed to their environment of light and air, the leaves take on a little color and an exquisitely smooth texture, and then stretch into horizontal, hand-shaped leaflets. This miracle continues for about three weeks, until they reach full

This dead conifer branch seems every bit as alive as the dogwood when brought inside.

The old wood from which we constructed the breakfront in the cabin was originally used in the Beaulieu Winery.

size. I've been watching the native buckeyes leaf out for more than twenty years, but I still become excited every spring when these startling chartreuse leaves appear. I love the "newness of green," that fresh green of grass, and the amazing palette of green hues trees produce in their new leaves. They seem to have a light of their own.

You can bring all sorts of swelling buds indoors —oaks and maples, birch, locust, mulberry—so that you can watch the miracle up close, day in and day out. In early spring, buckeyes sprout lovely pale cream-colored blossoms at the tips of the branches. It's best to cut them just as the tassels appear, so that they'll last for two or three weeks as the buds open into sweet-scented flowers. In the Napa Valley, they're called Roman candle trees, because the plume-shaped blossoms make the tree appear to be a giant candelabrum.

THE SELECTION IS THE ARRANGEMENT

Gathering branches isn't as tidy or precise as visiting a florist's shop. But it's a lot more spontaneous, creative, and fun. The pleasure of making nature's bouquets comes from the doing—the walking or hiking, the looking, the finding, the gathering and placing in a new place. No stuffy rules of flower "arrangement" need limit you—the selection is the arrangement. Often, nature's discards make the best ornaments. A large broken limb from an oak tree,

with its dramatic zigzag branches covered with moss and lichen, has already been designed and needs only to be placed elegantly on the mantel.

The birds are an ongoing role model and inspiration for me. When you examine any bird's nest, you see the thrift, ingenuity, and beauty of using "found objects" to create a home. The nesting instinct is just that —an instinct. When I gather branches, seeds, cones, and the like to bring home for my nest, I feel as though I'm part of some grander plan for homebuilding. And as I go reconnoitering for natural materials, I'm also reminded of the young Indian boy whose mother taught him to pat the earth each morning and apologize for the need to walk upon it.

FIELDS AND MEADOWS

*Now I see the secret
of the making of the best
persons. It is to grow
in the open air, and to eat
and sleep with the earth.*

WALT WHITMAN

e haven't had many poets come visit Pritchard Hill.

Or perhaps we have. My experience with poets is limited, but I've always suspected they come disguised as gardeners or great cooks. Or as Brownies— the little-girl variety. I learned much of what I know about the magic of fields and meadows from Brownies. From Troop 47, to be precise.

When my daughters Carissa and Alexa were young and members of Troop 47, we used to plan Brownie picnics that began at our house and ended in a wonderful open meadow. I was the "pack mule" for these outings. The procession of little girls, each carrying a basket for treasure-collecting, would leave our house in high spirits. They ran—through the vineyard, out the gate of the seven-foot deer fence, and into the wilds. For the first few miles, we followed an old dirt road through cool, still madrone and oak forests. The baskets were light because they were empty in the beginning. Except for mine, of course, loaded down with sandwiches, cookies, and fruit.

For the first hour, I had to hurry to keep up with all that Brownie energy and excitement. They'd call and shout to each other as they found treasures of all kinds— a cone, an interesting rock, a feather, dried moss, seedpods, lichen-covered sticks—and tucked them away in the baskets.

*H*idden in the meadow
marshes are the
bullfrogs. Sounding like a
tympani-and-tuba
concert, they begin their
song at twilight.
Their deep, melodious
beat sets up vibrations to
rival a rock concert.
Cattails provide a perfect
home for the bullfrogs,
but since they can
soon take over a pond, we
cut the reeds and the
cattails at the green stage
to use indoors.

BEAUTIFUL EARTH IN THREE MONTHS

Vegetable leftovers are a perfect addition to this compost recipe. Unlike natural woodlands and grassy meadows, our cultivated soil gets depleted because we take away what would in nature be returned as a home for bacteria, earthworms, fungi, and protozoans. Therefore, gardeners must replenish their soil and this is a simple way to do that.

1. Make a 6-inch-high layer of green materials—leaves, grass, etc.
2. Spread 2 inches of fresh cow, horse, or other manure on top of that.
3. Add a ½-inch layer of gypsum (dolomite).
4. Spread ¾ inch of potassium together with phosphate rock or bone meal in a thin layer.
5. Finish with 2 inches of good live topsoil.

Combined, this will be approximately 11 inches deep. Repeat this recipe three times, making a flat-topped pyramid about 30 inches high. Make a "moat" around the perimeter to hold water. Pour water over the top of the heap until it soaks thoroughly to the bottom.

After a week, turn over the whole pile and continue turning every two or three weeks. For three weeks after that, soak once a week. For a month after that, soak every two weeks. For the next two months, soak once a month.

I usually make the bottom layer about 4 by 6 feet. Do not use a box or pit, but work on open ground, as air is essential to the process.

Remember that air, moisture, and moderate outdoor temperature are all necessary for the rapid breakdown of the manure and other organic materials and for the active participation of the crucial organisms.

HOBO'S PICNIC, OR NO-LITTER LUNCH

Sandwich a tomato slice and a leaf of basil between two thick slices of Armenian or English cucumber. Wrap in a grape leaf or two, securing with a chive.

Make a "health food" sandwich of peanut butter, raisins, mayonnaise, and lettuce on your favorite bread. Wrap in a large grape or cabbage leaf and tie up with a parsley stem.

Place a strip of sun-dried tomato and a slice of chicken between two sticks of celery and slip a ½-inch ring of long, narrow purple pepper around them to hold together.

Include a piece of fruit or raw vegetable, even a raw baby ear of corn in its own husk.

Slit the skin of a banana, part slightly to add drips of melted chocolate, and cover with granola. Close the skin again.

Place all the goodies in the center of a bandanna and tie the corners over a stick. Place stick over your shoulder and proceed on your hike. Along the way, keep your eyes open for horsetail needles and mint.

Bring along a thermos of hot water, add two handfuls of horsetail needles (Equisetum arvense, usually found near water), and steep.

But soon, Brownie energy being what it is, the shouts turned, well, just a little whiny. They were hungry. They were tired. They were hot. The pack mule put on her cheerleading hat and urged them on. "When we come to a nice clearing, we'll stop."

Ahh—new energy would bubble forth. The hungriest would gather the others up and hurry them along to the perfect place. Always, always there was a perfect place. A warm, sweet-smelling, grassy meadow, shaded on at least one side by spreading trees.

Meadows are, above all, sensual places. They're places to stretch out and feel sun-warmed grass tickle the backs of your legs. Or, if you're hot, they're places to feel shade-cooled grass against a hot and sticky cheek. Wildflowers smell spicier, lemonade tastes sweeter, the homeliest peanut butter sandwich seems nothing short of ambrosia.

Brownies are too big for naps, of course; they've outgrown them. But after lunch, filled with sun and sandwiches, they'd get drowsy, curl up where they fell, and sleep. Even the cheerleader, far too grown-up for naps herself, might nod off under one of the dense oak trees that edge the meadow.

Now, years later, I remember those picnics with great pleasure. I remember the warm and open expanse of grass, and the beauty of the wildflowers, and I wonder if I ever thought to tell the Brownies that, as writer Loren Eiseley reminds us, "flowers changed the world."

WAKE UP, WAKE UP!
IT'S I WHO WANT YOU FOR COMPANION,
SLEEPING BUTTERFLY!
—*MATSUO BASHO*

One hundred million years ago, there were no flowers on the face of the earth. It took what Darwin called "an abominable mystery," an explosion of the angiosperms, or flowering plants, for flowers to appear on the planet. There were reptiles on the earth, but no birds sang in the forests, no warm-blooded mammals called the earth home.

As Eiseley points out,

> *The agile brain of the warm-blooded birds and mammals demands a high oxygen consumption and food in concentrated forms, or the creatures cannot long sustain themselves. It was the rise of the flowering plants that provided that energy and changed the nature of the living world. Their appearance parallels in a quite surprising manner the rise of the birds and mammals.*

When the breeze stirred in the meadow, I thought of the angiosperms, seeds tucked inside, caught by the wind and sent spinning out to reproduce themselves—beautiful, fruitful, and changing the face of the earth.

Plant a wildflower window box using the wildflowers of your area—here in California, we plant dwarf lupine, California poppies, baby blue eyes, Rocky Mountain penstemon, pink oxalis, matricaria, African daisies, candytuft, Johnny-jump-ups, and creeping zinnias to trail down over the box.

BASIC FRESH GOAT CHEESE WITH HERBS

Put one gallon of goat's milk in a glass jar with a lid and close the lid.

Allow to stand in sun until curd and whey are clearly separated. Spoon out the curd into cheesecloth. Let hang for one or two days under a shady tree, until the bag is not dripping with whey. Put cheese into a mixing bowl and add your favorite dried herbs, salt, pepper, and garlic to taste. My favorite herb recipe includes lots of oregano, some basil, and a little lemon thyme, plus fresh garlic, a dash of cayenne, and a pinch of salt.

Allow to sit for several hours or several days in the refrigerator. The herb and garlic flavors will strengthen with time.

THE PLEASURE OF "GETTING THERE"

As any parent knows, there comes a time when you are not automatically included in your children's outings. That's part of the rhythm of child-raising, that bittersweet period when their ability to see themselves and think of themselves as independent human beings is inhibited by the presence of someone who has the title "Mom" or "Dad" rather than a name.

That time came with all my children, of course. But, even in the midst of that terrible transition we call adolescence, there were times when one of them wanted me to take part in something he or she had planned.

With my middle son, there were expeditions to the place we called "Jon-Mark's Meadow." It was not an easy journey there—the way involved six miles up and down very steep, rocky mountainsides. There was scratchy underbrush along the way, and just to make sure only the stout of heart and leg made it to the meadow, there were poison oak and snakes, too.

So thick were the manzanitas and chaparral that the way never seemed clear to me. I was at the mercy of a young Natty Bumppo, my own twelve-year-old pathfinder. You'd think a mother being invited as a guest on this kind of journey would be grateful and gracious. Well, I wasn't—not always. I complained—of the heat, the exertion, the length of the hike.

But Jon-Mark knew a journey worth taking. When we finally arrived at his meadow, lush and open, surrounded by stands of eucalyptus trees, carpeted with green grass and wildflowers, no sight had ever been lovelier or more welcome. Jon-Mark's meadow invited me in, in a warm, sunny way the woods and boulders could not offer. While Jon-Mark ventured off to the river to catch a trout or two, I would settle in with a book or a notepad and feel all the world fresh and joyous before me.

OPEN HEARTS, OPEN SPACES

Fields and meadows serve very practical purposes, of course. They provide grazing land for deer and cattle, room for young spring animals to stretch their legs and learn independence, and a perfectly structured ecological system that unites birds, bees, and wildflowers in their transitory cycles.

Today, when I hear or read debates about open spaces, I think back to Jon-Mark's meadow. I believe open spaces, wide, grassy fields and meadows, are as necessary to us as food or shelter. The sky is both wider and nearer in a meadow. The strong, beautiful horizontal lines of an open field are the best antidote for the relentless verticals with which we live—skyscrapers and their ilk. In urban areas, it sometimes seems wasteful to preserve a wide-open field just for the pleasure of it.

FAMILY DRESSING RECIPES

Homemade bread and whole vegetables from the garden give guests the opportunity to create their own sandwiches or salad, choosing from a variety of dressings.

DOMINIC'S CREAMY HERB SAUCE
Homemade mayonnaise
Minced garlic
Fresh chopped tarragon
Dijon mustard
Shallots, finely diced
Fresh ground pepper

DONN'S SPECIAL
Our homemade wine vinegar
(which is a blend of 1 part red
wine to 3 parts white wine and
aged for months)
Sherry and balsamic vinegar
Napa Valley virgin olive oil
Salt and pepper

CYRIL'S ORIENTAL TWIST
Peanut oil
Olive oil
Rice-wine vinegar
Soy sauce
Fresh ground pepper

LYGIA'S PURE AND SIMPLE
Dry mustard
Lemon juice
Homemade wine vinegar
Hazelnut or walnut oil
Salt and pepper

WILD MEADOW SALAD

Go to the meadow with a bowl, some herb vinegar, virgin olive oil, and an appetite. Gather handfuls of miner's lettuce and watercress. Pick a few leaves of dock, mallow, dandelion, mint, mustard, and several mustard flowers. Mix, dress, and eat with your fingers.

Meadows are not just for visitors who want to picnic, fling themselves in the grass, lie on their backs, and spin stories about the cloud-pictures up above. Without those generous spaces, we'd never really experience the fragile beauty of the natural world. And without that experience, we could not hold it in the reverence we must if we are to preserve the earth for our children and our children's children. As writer Steve van Matre points out, "We must learn to love ourselves less and the earth more." I believe those are simply two facets of the same love. And nothing reminds me of that more than the Easter mornings we've spent on Pritchard Hill.

A VINEYARD ON A VERY FRUITFUL HILL

Many families have traditions tied to spring holidays—coloring Easter eggs, hiding a piece of matzo on the first two nights of Passover. In our family, tradition gets us up very early on Easter morning. That's the day we, along with a few close friends and their children, head to the top of Pritchard Hill for a breakfast picnic at dawn.

In the Napa Valley, it's still chilly on most spring mornings. So we bundle up, and, while it's still dark, load the jeep with the makings of a favorite family breakfast, and send our procession up the hill—on foot, on bikes, on horses, and, for those past hiking, by jeep.

Certain rituals await us at the top of the hill. The Easter Bunny has always been up before anyone else, hiding eggs for the young. But before the hunt, before Donn's delicious scrambled Easter eggs, thirty-six to a pan over an open fire, each picnic participant must share a special reading with the rest of us.

You can imagine the variety of inspirational messages we've had over the years, everything from Japanese haiku to Mary Baker Eddy. The smallest members of the party usually volunteer "There is not a spot where God is not." But one reading stays with me still. It was the morning our late friend Anne Baxter read to us just as dawn was breaking. The children were in that half-awake state between drowse and wiggles, straining their eyes through the dim light to see if they could catch sight of a brightly colored egg hiding amid the lupine, buttercups, Indian paintbrush, and California poppies. But even the youngest stilled as Anne's glorious voice washed over the meadow around us. She chose to read the fifth chapter of Isaiah.

Now will I sing to my wellbeloved a song of my beloved touching his vineyard. My wellbeloved hath a vineyard in a very fruitful hill: And he fenced it, and gathered out the stones thereof, and planted it with the choicest vine, and built a tower in the midst of it, and also made a winepress therein: and he looked that it should bring forth grapes, and it brought forth wild grapes.

CLAIRE'S MUSTARD MOUSSE

Donn's sister, Claire, makes this mustard mousse, a great accompaniment to Easter ham.

4 eggs
⅔ cup sugar
1 tablespoon unflavored gelatin
1 tablespoon dry mustard
1 ½ tablespoons Napa Valley mustard (hot sweet)
½ teaspoon turmeric
¼ teaspoon salt
1 cup water
½ cup cider vinegar
1 cup whipping cream

Beat eggs in top of a double boiler and set aside. Mix the sugar and gelatin thoroughly in a bowl; in another bowl combine mustards, turmeric, and salt. Add water and vinegar to the eggs, stir in the sugar mixture, and cook, stirring constantly, over boiling water until completely dissolved. Cool to room temperature, then whip the cream and stir into the mixture.

Turn into a 1 ½-quart mold and chill until set. Unmold by dipping in hot water for a few seconds.

Serves 8–10

Purchase a packing blanket from a moving company. Cut a large cardboard stencil for one quarter of an abstract flower of your own design. Lay the stencil on one corner of the blanket and paint. Rotate the stencil from quadrant to quadrant, painting each section, until the design is complete.

After breakfast, there's always music—a guitar or two, usually some singing, and a flute on occasion.

Sitting there, with my beloved family and friends, it is impossible not to give myself up to the celebration and peace of the day.

There are boulders below us, woods around us, and, sloping down the hill, well-ordered vineyards. But there, atop Pritchard Hill, we revel in the grand openness of the meadow. And remind ourselves, for yet another year, that the most precious treasures in this life are free for the taking. Enjoying the morning, the music, our friends and family, I wonder to myself, why do we gather like this only on Easter morning?

THE CULTIVATED GARDEN

On Pritchard Hill, the dominant colors are the greens of the vineyard, surrounded by gray-blue oaks on lavender hills, and lots of blue sky above. In our cultivated garden, we've introduced variations of these colors to harmonize with the surrounding hues. In late summer, when the sun lowers on the horizon and bathes everything in a soft, warm light, stronger colors seem necessary. We bring in bright yellow, orange, and rust flowers to harmonize with the amber, copper, and gold of the oaks, maples, and grapevines. So that our winery would seem a natural part of this special environment, we designed it in a pyramidal shape to repeat the form of one particular hill directly behind the building. The roof of the winery is made of steel, which forms a protective rust coating that mimics our reddish earth. Slowly, I've come to realize that the best cultivation, whether in the garden or in life, is being able to "see through," the ability to look beyond, beyond troubles, adolescence, illness, to a greater vision. The woods have helped me see that there is value in understanding the concept of foreground, middle ground, and distant vista. The interruptions of the overall view only enhance the ultimate view. Cultivation is work, to be sure. That is what sets it apart from the benign neglect of the wild garden. But it is work that gives peace, harmony, bounty, and the one unmistakable feeling that you are a caretaker of this fragile blue-green jewel we call the Earth.

The Cultivated Garden

Surrounded—and inspired—by the beauty of the wild garden, I had only to look, listen, smell, feel, and pay attention to know how to plan and cultivate a garden here on Pritchard Hill. When we first moved here, plenty of beauty surrounded us. In fact, only the man-made parts of our environment were less than beautiful. That was an important early lesson. By taking our cues from nature over the years, we have tried to plant in harmony with our surroundings. Nature is still the best designer, incorporating open spaces and shaded woods with hard, sculptural shapes. I try to include this variety in our garden, remembering Alexander Pope's counsel in his epistle to Lord Burlington: "Consult the Genius of the Place." Today, when I take in the vista from our hilltop, I see a gentleness to the entire landscape. Serenity is important to me—to all of us, I think—and that's the feeling created by the vineyard, encircled by rolling hills with mountains behind. On a clear day, we can see seven ranges of mountains from our terrace. In the vegetable garden, we've tried to reflect those gentle swells and curves, looking for symmetry not in rectangles or regimented rows but in gradual, sweeping curves. We've designed paths as nature would, letting them find their own course, and using materials we've found in our environment—wood chips, grape seeds, flagstones from the hillside, and river-washed gravel. We've also tried to learn the lessons the natural world has to offer about color.

THE VINEYARD

*And they shall build
houses, and inhabit them;
and they shall plant
vineyards, and eat the
fruit of them.*

ISAIAH 65:21

The approach to our house and to the winery winds through acres of dark, cool woods. If you're driving, it's really just a few miles from the main road to our entry. But the way seems longer, winding over the weather-roughened road. Suddenly, there you are—in the sunlight, looking out on row upon row of grapevines laid out on the hillside. Even though I've made the journey thousands of times, I still get a thrill when I come upon the vineyard, an unexpected sign of civilization.

Our journey here actually began many years before we set eyes on Pritchard Hill. For most of his adult life, Donn had been studying, tasting, and collecting wines. And the more he knew, the more he began to think that he'd like to turn his hand to making a world-class wine.

Then, about twenty-five years ago, his dream began to take shape. Everything he'd read and heard led him to believe that the best wines in the world come from hillside vineyards with seemingly unfriendly, rocky, gravelly soil.

One day in 1966, when we had just begun our search for the perfect property, Donn met with André Tchelistcheff, the dean of American winemakers. André confirmed Donn's belief. He said, "If you really want to make great wine, go to the hills." He had a caveat, of course. "Farming will cost you more," he warned, "but it will be worth it."

And so it has been.

THE PROTEAN VINE

Vineyards have to be the most beautiful form of agriculture. They have the linear quality I love in other forms of row crops. And they have a unique advantage: you don't have to replant them each season, and they stay green all summer without water. Grapes have a life span much like that of the humans who tend them. With care and some good fortune, vines can live for a hundred years or so. In fact, most viticulturists believe grapevines keep improving up to about thirty years before they reach a plateau. Of course, we like to think people keep improving longer than that—three score and ten, or more.

Whatever the individual grapevine's form—whether trellised, espaliered, or head-pruned to form a bush—a wonderful design emerges when you step back and look at row upon row of vines in a vineyard. The pattern comes not just from the planted rows, but from the diagonal rows that appear as the trunks line up in several directions.

Besides the geometric design, the relationship of vines to land is revealing. When working in or walking through our vineyard, one has a strong sense of the up-and-down contour of the land—you realize there's scarcely a level square foot as the vines come over the hills and define and accent the rhythm of the terrain.

*Though their real purpose
is to provide
protection and food for the
grapes, grape leaves
are also useful to people as
decoration and food.
The colorful fall leaves,
when cut, will last
for several days if properly
conditioned by
sprinkling with water,
sealing them in a plastic
bag, and storing in the
refrigerator.*

THE SEASONS OF THE GRAPES

Each stage of growing offers a new kind of visual excitement. In winter, you see the quiet strength of the vines, vulnerable without their splendid adornment of leaves. When the vines have lost their fall show of spectacular color, they appear dark and gnarled, silhouetted against the gray winter sky.

The coldest season of the year means it's time to begin the long, slow process of pruning. This is not a production-line task. Instead, every single vine must be pruned according to its individual needs. The weather is often freezing cold or rainy, and even well-gloved hands have a hard time squeezing the clippers. The days are short, the light is dim, and the sun is low on the horizon.

After weeks of winter rains, a few warm days creep into the calendar and the mustard appears, luring us into a mistaken belief that spring must be here. Not yet. Instead, I'm sure the real reason for the sudden pre-spring surprise of mustard is so that we can stand back from our work for a few moments and admire the way the golden yellow sets off the dark sculptural beauty of the vines.

There's a lovely sense of community, living and working in our agricultural region, where the buzz of conversation is always about the vines and the weather. We all have our eyes and ears (and hearts and pocket-books) tuned to Mother Nature. Around February, everyone knows when the buds start to swell. We're all waiting for March and budbreak.

There is a quiet peacefulness when winter comes to the Napa Valley. The dormant vines enjoy the cold, but when spring comes and tender new shoots appear, freezing temperatures can be disastrous.

Sometimes I feel as if we need a musical composition about the progress of the vines, piped through the streets, letting the visitors know what's really going on in the vineyard. The music might have its dark or melancholy moments as well. One of the vintner's great worries is that the temperature will drop below freezing during the early growth of new, tender shoots. This can damage or destroy not only those exquisite fresh green leaves but an entire year's crop. When we first moved to the valley, the main method of confronting an untimely spring frost was with the heat of "smudge pots." These small metal stoves heated by diesel fuel were placed on every row to heat the air around the vines. Now we use more effective—and ecologically sound—wind machines or overhead sprinklers, which form a protective coating of ice around each branch. As you can imagine, frost alerts make for restless nights. Since we're a hillside vineyard, we enjoy a little more security from frost—the cool air flows downhill, leaving us safer than valley vineyards.

Of course, most people welcome spring, that fresh, bright beginning after winter's chill. But in the wine country, you can almost read spring on people's faces as they watch, once again, the miracle of the vines, the light green leaves multiplying daily as the vines creep out in all directions.

It's a kind of hope and joy that marks spring growth, but the mood that strikes near harvest time is different—anticipatory and full of excitement.

To echo the wood, metal, and glass
of winery equipment, we designed our first
dinner inside the winery in the early 1970s
for some of our special customers.
Empty barrels became table bases, pallets were
tabletops, and hose clamps our napkin rings.

There's a wonderful—and wonderfully efficient—underground network in a rural area. If anyone is having a problem or needs an extra tractor, the word goes out and soon the problem is solved. When we first moved to the Napa Valley we didn't know a single soul. We were newcomers and competitors, and yet when we needed help, help poured in from every quarter.

Our first vintage, 1968, is a fine example of the harmony and cooperation among the vintners in those early days. Because our winery was not yet complete, Joe Heitz offered to crush our grapes and turn them into wine. Robert Mondavi offered to bottle the wine, and Jack Davies of Schramsberg volunteered to store it in his caves. I've always felt that particular vintage should be labeled "The Spirit of Napa Valley."

THE FARMER IN HIS ROCKY DELL

Grape growers are, of course, farmers, engaged in a form of agriculture so venerable it was already old news in the Old Testament. Like all agricultural pursuits, growing grapes is hard, labor-intensive work. In our vineyard, we handle—that is, literally handle by hand—each of the sixty thousand grapevines six times a year. Each vine has to be pruned, suckered, tied, hand-fertilized (custom-fed, according to each plant's needs), retied, and then picked. What about

machines, you might wonder? The steep terraces make
the use of any kind of automatic picking machine out
of the question.

Having come from an urban area with air and
water pollution problems, we could perhaps better
appreciate the need to care for the environment than
the people who had lived only in the clean air of the
country. Even in the early years here at Pritchard Hill,
we bought ladybugs and lacewings as predators of the
whitefly and leafhopper in order to avoid spraying.

I well remember the refrigerator being full of
boxes of lacewings waiting for the exact moment when
the leafhopper nymphs would emerge. Then we set the
lacewings free to do their job. We also removed all the
coffeeberry bushes (host plants for whiteflies) from
the entire perimeter of the vineyard.

We were one of the first Napa Valley vineyards
to use a ground cover in place of disking between the
rows of grapevines. The low-growing Zorro fescue does
not rob the nutrients from the vines while it keeps
our precious earth from eroding and the moisture from
evaporating. It also acts as an alternate host for both
pests and predator insects. At present, we are working
with the University of California at Davis on developing
a totally organic farming program.

In our family, everyone was part of the process
of grape growing. In the early days, Donn was on the
tractor from dawn's first light until dark. There were
plenty of chores for the children—hoeing, picking,
pruning. We pruned in the rain and picked when 110-

In 1971, at age three, young Dominic eagerly learns to cut the ripe clusters from a cabernet sauvignon vine.

GRAPE GOULASH

One of the children's all-time favorites is sour cream and grapes—covered with brown sugar and set in the refrigerator. For company, we serve the grape goulash in chilled bittersweet chocolate cups or in a precooked almond-coconut crust.

degree sun scorched us. The grapes, like time and the tide, wait for no man—or woman or child. To make the best wine, the grapes must be picked at the exact moment when the sugar and acid are in perfect balance for that particular wine. Summer comes late in our part of Northern California, so often it was the hottest day of the year when we needed to pick our grapes. One particularly memorable harvest, the temperature soared to 112 degrees. Hats, plenty of water, and, for me, a wet kerchief on my neck were survival resources.

You can begin to feel the realness of picking only after a full day in the blazing sun. After bending and stooping in unaccustomed positions, it becomes almost impossible to straighten up. Every single muscle aches, from neck to toe. Adding to that discomfort is the thick coating of sticky grape juice, dust, and good old-fashioned sweat that covers all exposed skin—hands, arms, and face. And of course picking is never over in a day. It goes on for weeks sometimes, six to ten days in a row without a break. When the grapes are ripe, they don't wait—whatever made us think we were in charge of this operation? It is the grapes that dictate to us all year long—when to be pruned, when to be tied, when to be picked, etc., etc., etc.

And yet, lest I've painted too bleak a picture, there is great beauty, satisfaction, and pleasure in the harvest. The sound of beautiful Mexican folk songs echoing in our natural amphitheater and the sound of the children's constant barbs, laughter, and teasing keep the arduous picking from being unrelievedly grim.

THE TABLEVINE

Making a grapevine stand up is really quite simple if you have Redi-mix cement.

Redi-mix cement
Water
Pure pigments: sienna, raw umber, black
Stick about the size of a pencil
Interestingly shaped grapevine, including part of trunk
Large metal or glass pie plate

Mix half a bucket of cement with a little water and brown and black pigments. Stir colors well. Adjust color to match trunk of grapevine. Holding vine upright in the middle of pie plate, pour colored cement around the base, up to about 3 inches from bottom of trunk. Begin forming the cement with your hands into root-like fingers, as it sets up quickly. Keep forming the shape until firm. Immediately comb with stick or your fingertips to simulate trunk's texture. After cement has thoroughly set, gently twist long cane (the arm that comes off the trunk of the vine) into a rhythmic pattern. Decorating with grapes is optional.

Each year, when the harvest ends, I try to reflect on some of the extra pleasures of growing grapes: the sheer beauty of living in the middle of a vineyard, with its ever-changing magnificent visual displays; the wonderful feeling of being part of American agriculture, of growing something useful; and the gift of being able to carry what we grow to a beautiful conclusion—wine.

When I think about these pleasures, I remember something Hugh Johnson wrote:

For all the style and glamour of its market image, its roots are in the earth . . . Wine is one of the miracles of nature, and . . . its 10,000 years of partnership with man has not removed that element of mystery, that independent life that alone among all our foods has made men think of it as divine.

WORKING FOR THE DIVINE

If we were just selling our grapes, we might prune and feed and water to produce a larger crop. However, since our concern is not with tonnage but with producing the most intensely flavorful grape, our viticultural practices and choice of soil, mountainside, rootstock, and fruiting wood are critical.

Bradley Ogden, chef/owner of Lark Creek Inn, at work in the vineyard.

From the time of budbreak to the moment of harvest, every aspect of the weather—heat, rain, wind, fog—affects that vintage. This is why no two vintages are exactly alike. Two extreme examples come to mind—1976 and 1982.

Nineteen seventy-six was a drought year. The grapevines were feeling stressed from lack of water and produced only a small crop. The summer ripening weather was ideal—long, even temperatures of warm days and cool nights from verasion (the period when the berries soften a bit and start to sugar up and when the red grapes begin to turn color) to harvest. The cabernet grapes were particularly intense in flavor and produced a big wine that matured slowly.

In direct contrast to 1976 was 1982, when an extraordinary amount of rain fell, producing lush growth and heavy crops. That year the cabernet was lighter and ready to drink earlier than our previous cabernets. Same vines, same care; very different wines.

As farmers, we can never forget the weather. One of the reasons so many people come here to make wine is that the Napa Valley offers very special climatic conditions required by *Vitis vinifera*, the wine grape. During the summer heat, the coastal fogs come into the Napa Valley at night and lower the temperature as much as forty degrees. On our hill, we even have a climate slightly different from the one on the valley floor. While we benefit from the cooling effect and moisture of the fog, at seventeen hundred feet we're often above the fog,

and our grapes ripen a bit earlier. Nineteen seventy-five illustrates the climatic differences between the valley floor and the hillside vineyards. All summer, the fog settled in the valley and prevented the ripening of grapes. Then the rains came and many unripened grapes rotted on the vine. Sitting in sunshine above the fog, our grapes ripened nicely to produce one of our best vintages.

In the Napa Valley, everybody celebrates the end of harvest. The parties we have are ways to express joy, to mark the finale of a year's work, and to thank all who have participated in the harvest, including the powers that be. At our vineyard, we used to cook up a storm and throw a big party for the workers who had helped us all year long. But one fall, I got sick during the harvest. To my delight, the workers got together, cooked a marvelous Mexican feast, and treated us to a party. We've continued the tradition—we fund the party and the workers do the cooking. We decorate the crushing area with piñatas, bright banners, and four-foot balloons for the children. We all enjoy good food, music, and great wine; and we begin thinking about the year ahead.

THERE'S A HUSH THAT FALLS OVER EVERYONE
WHO ENTERS OUR WINERY. PERHAPS THAT'S WHY,
WHEN HUGH JOHNSON FIRST SAW THE WINERY,
HE DESCRIBED IT AS A "CATHEDRAL OF WINE."

Donn tastes the current vintage of cabernet from the barrel. He is always happy to share with guests the older vintages. Of course the first question is always "Which are your favorites?" And although it's a bit like asking a parent which child he or she likes best, Donn will tell guests that the 1969 early on set a bench mark for us and helped establish our reputation. It's still a great wine and has a good life ahead. Donn confesses, however, to liking the 1970 equally well. The 1975 is a big favorite with many people. It's a beautiful wine and very smooth, but Donn prefers the more full-bodied wine of the 1976. The 1977 illustrates so clearly how a wine goes on living and changing until the day it's consumed. Not outstanding for the first ten years or so, it is delightful to drink today. In 1980 Donn decided to identify remarkable vintages with his signature. The 1980 and 1984 through 1987 all are recent wines that have been exceptional and bear his signature.

Seeing the result of an entire year's work come to fruition isn't just a phrase; where we live, it's what keeps us working day in and day out. Our 1969 cabernet, which for eight years held the world's record for the highest price paid for a single bottle of American wine, was the realization of Donn's dream. Not because it was a "high-priced pour" (although that was certainly nice), but because it was a memorable expression of the vintner's art.

Winemaking represents a collaboration of farmer, artist, and scientist, sometimes all inhabiting one body. In our vineyard, we're fortunate to have three talented individuals—a viticulturist, an enologist, and Donn, the artist—to round out the team.

There is, as Hugh Johnson points out, something quite "divine" about wine, perhaps because it comes from a process of natural fermentation or because its clean flavor and crisp acidity provide such a perfect counterpoint to food. When used in cooking, wine does magical things. Just as herbs and spices bring out the flavor of certain foods, so it is with wine. In cooking, the alcohol in wine virtually disappears, leaving only the unparalleled essence of aged grape juice to enhance the dish. Once you start experimenting with using wine in cooking, you want to put it in every dish, and I do— except hot cereal and waffles. All you need is an adventuresome spirit and a fairly good wine. Remember that the better the wine, the better the dish.

Wine seems, as an accompaniment to food, to cut the richness of fat and helps us assimilate nutrients in food, not to mention making even the most ordinary meal a feast. Some ordinary dishes that wine has turned into feasts for us are mussels with chenin blanc, spinach and pine nuts with chardonnay, lamb and basmati rice or aged Jack cheese with cabernet, a salad of smoked chicken, persimmon, and sunflower seeds with Riesling, and Donn's favorite, tuna sandwiches with Riesling. The excitement of discovering new combinations that make both the wine and the food seem more interesting is what it's all about. Sometimes it's finding wines that have components similar to the food's; other times, it's enjoying contrasting components. But at its most poetic, wine represents a product that truly transcends time, place, material, and, of course, human effort.

I try to create that same poetic feeling that transcends place when I design special wine-tasting events. Because I think of a cellar as a magical and seductive place, I've sometimes wanted to re-create those feelings far, far away from our own cellar. For the California Barrel Tasting at the Stanford Court Hotel in San Francisco, we virtually transformed a lower-level ballroom into a wine cellar with 130 sixty-gallon barrels and magnificent gnarled grapevine sculptures. It wasn't just the look we were after; it was the touch of wood, the rich, musty smell, and the taste, of course, that we wanted as well.

For one California Barrel Tasting dinner at the Stanford Court Hotel in San Francisco, we collected many different-size small barrels to use as centerpieces. Some antique barrels were used, but most were newly assembled in the Napa Valley. Some of the ends were pushed out to enable us to light the interiors. Rounds from smaller barrels were used for table numbers, and champagne corks were used to hold place cards.

The barrel theme was emphasized by the empty sixty-gallon oak barrels we transported from our winery to the Stanford Court foyer. Getting them into the freight elevator and down the narrow corridors was no small feat. The results were worth it. By the time the guests reached the stairway to the foyer, the aroma of wood and wine transported them into the ballroom.

From the picking perspective, I have seen and loved the hanging jewel-like bunches of grapes for years. To share this point of view with others, I designed huge bunches of "grapes" to hang overhead at the California barrel tasting.

After the event, we moved the giant grape bunches eighty miles away to the Napa Valley. We were able to store them in a cool, dark area while they waited for their next glamorous appearance. The opening of Vintner's Village in St. Helena was the perfect occasion. This time their performance was outside in a more appropriate place—under a real grape arbor.

THE IMAGINARY PLAYGROUND

When our children were growing up, the vineyards also created a kind of extended playground. They saw the vines as row upon row of wonderful pathways for their horseback rides or minibike adventures. We had a number of serious conversations about what was—and was not—permitted, imbuing the youngest members of the household with respect for the vines. Minibikes were only permitted on the perimeter of the vineyard.

The horses were welcome only with their riders, and then only at certain times of the year. Winter was okay, except after a rain, because the horses' hooves would pack down the soil. Early spring was marginal, we told the children. They could ride only if they could control the horse and keep him from snacking on the tender vine shoots. Summer was out of the question, because the dust was so thick that, when stirred up, it would coat the leaves and prevent the plant from breathing. Fall was best, after the grapes were picked and before the rains started.

Whether it was mud or dust, I often wondered how there could be any dirt left for the vines out of doors, since it seemed as if every last speck found its way into the house. During the early summers, when there wasn't yet much of a green barrier between vineyard and house, the children would come inside covered head to toe with a reddish-brown dust that seemed glued on.

CHENIN BLANC SORBET

Sequoia makes her simplified version of this sorbet by simply freezing a bunch of chenin blanc grapes and eating them just as they thaw.

2½ pounds green grapes (preferably chenin blanc)
1 cup Chappellet (dry) chenin blanc
⅓ cup sugar
Fresh grape leaves
Small clusters of green grapes, with leaves, for garnish

Chop grapes in a food processor in batches, using 10 on/off turns. Push pulp through a strainer into a measuring cup until you have 3 cups of grape juice. Set aside. Heat wine and sugar in a small saucepan over low heat, swirling pan occasionally, until sugar dissolves. Increase heat and bring just to a boil, then remove from heat and cool to room temperature.

Combine reserved grape juice and cooled syrup in a bowl, then freeze in an ice-cream maker. Serve immediately, or place in freezer for several hours to mellow flavors. Spoon into goblets and garnish with grape clusters.

Alexandra and Max play in the giant's basket, a playhouse made from dormant grapevines. Mustard is abundant in springtime vineyards, and they use it to decorate the walls and roof of their outdoor castle.

The same principles apply, whether you are making a giant basket or a picnic-size basket— if the vines get too brittle, soak them in water until they are supple enough to weave through the supports. Vertical supports can be any material—from steel reinforcing bars to support giant baskets, to small tree branches for picnic baskets.

MORE THAN GRAPES

I've learned to see everything about the vineyard as useful in multiple ways. Old, broken stakes aren't discarded; when they can't do service any longer in the vineyard, we recycle them. They've become stakes for the vegetable garden, been hammered into trellises, been used as fences, served as ceiling wood in our cabin and as slats in my greenhouse, and even been turned into bases for our winery desks.

The grapevines themselves, dark and twisted, are amenable to all sorts of uses. We make grapevine baskets from prunings, use grapevines as Christmas trees, or simply enjoy the unique shape of a vine as a sculpture. We use grape pumice (seeds and skins left after the pressing) as a ground cover in the fruit orchard and rose garden. This rich black topping is a pleasure to see and to walk on, and it keeps the weeds down like nothing else.

The country feeling in our cabin is enhanced by using old beams and broken grape stakes on the ceiling. Handsplit redwood stakes also make a handsome bouquet.

*F*ree-form topiaries of
live grapevines
transplanted into silver
wine coolers adorn a
formal setting arranged for
Susan Robbins at the
Spring Mountain Winery
(where television's
"Falcon Crest" was taped).
The larger grapevine
on the mantel is growing
in its own terra-cotta pot.

*W*hen the glass container
is left partially empty,
both grapes and glass
retain a sculptural quality.

THE GENEROUS EARTH

O ccasionally, despite all evidence to the contrary, we forget that the work of growing grapes is really only a consulting assignment. We can intervene, we can help things along, but, like all farmers and gardeners, we are dependent on the generosity of the earth itself. Which is to say that we are not nearly as important as we think we are.

Since we don't irrigate, rainfall is always a concern. Mild temperatures and too much humidity can sprout mold and mildew. Strong winds can snap tender young shoots. If there's too much heat or rain during the flowering, shattering will take place, allowing only a small percentage of berries to set. The grapes have enemies—diseases, various insects, and other pests. The list is long—and frightening.

Every year, we are reminded that the cultivated garden is not so different from the wild garden after all. We feel doubly blessed when our efforts and nature's come together to make wonderful wine. When I look back at the worries of drought, disease, or pests, and at the work we did to manage those worries, I understand again what is meant by "the wine of astonishment."

VEGETABLES

*My vegetable love
should grow
Vaster than empires,
and more slow.*

ANDREW MARVELL

Whendpeople come visit and look out at my acres of kitchen garden, and think about Donn and me pretty much living alone here, unless they're awfully shy they ask, "Molly, whatever could you have been thinking of? You must grow enough here to feed a small army."

Well, yes, I do. And once upon a time, I did feed a small army, day in and day out. An army of children with absolutely unfillable tummies, and an army of guests as well. And I fed them with vegetables that grew more quickly—and more satisfyingly—than the impatient Mr. Marvell could imagine.

As I look around the valley now, dotted with more than 250 wineries, it's hard to believe that in the late 1960s, when we came here, ours was only the second new winery established after Prohibition. Because of that, we were quite a curiosity to wine lovers, writers, and other visitors. And naturally, when people came all this way to see us, we had to feed them. In 1967, the most glamorous restaurant in St. Helena was the A&W, so entertaining meant entertaining at home. Most often, those were spur-of-the-moment meals, and often we were caught without a sufficient supply of food on hand. Clearly, we had to find a solution. With lots of children and little or no help, it was a challenge to make the trip to town. If the journey had been rewarded by magnificent fresh produce, I might have felt it was worth the effort of loading up the baby and several small children.

VEGETABLES

However, no car seats were required then, and the romping, squabbling, and general pandemonium that went on during the fifty-minute round trip were far more exhausting than a day's work in the garden.

Growing our own food became the solution. Here we were, living in the country with plenty of land on which to grow things and raise animals. Chickens were easy. The boys helped their father fence off the orchard and build a clever roosting house where we could collect eggs without disturbing the chickens. There were no volunteers willing to commit themselves to milking a cow twice a day, so we traded a neighbor wine for milk. Then the vegetables were planted. In the beginning, we had a small, strictly utilitarian garden. But soon the garden became a lifesaver. When unexpected guests popped in for lunch or dinner, I could walk into the garden and begin creating a meal. We all quickly discovered that nothing tastes quite as good as garden-grown vegetables, raised without chemicals or inorganic fertilizers and picked fresh. What began as a necessity grew into a passion.

Most of us begin relationships with vegetables when we are very young. If you grew up in a home where vegetables were overcooked to a suspicious and soggy gray-green mush, you may have waited until adulthood to fall in love with them. Today, when anyone mentions the word "vegetables," I think "beautiful" and my mind jumps to an image of a single vegetable, or to a home garden with vegetables all in a row, or to a huge agricultural field.

Greeted by the marvelous scent of the Casablanca lilies and an unexpected bouquet of onions on the front door, guests are predisposed to have a good time.

DONN'S WALLA WALLA ONION SANDWICH

When Donn won the Cook's *magazine "Who's Who" award, this is the recipe they chose to print.*

*2 slices corn-rye bread
Nutty peanut butter
Mayonnaise
¼-inch slice sweet Walla Walla onion*

Spread one slice of bread with a thick layer of mayonnaise. Spread the other slice with a thick layer of peanut butter.

Sandwich onion slice between pieces of bread and enjoy!

BEYOND SURVIVAL

One day, visiting my friend Maggie Wetzel in Alexander Valley, I suddenly saw what scale and imagination could do to a garden. Her vegetable garden, with its graceful curves, trellised vegetables, and well-defined paths, was more spectacular and imaginative than most flower gardens. I immediately contacted her landscape architect, Leland Noel, to ask for his counsel. After spending some time on Pritchard Hill, he presented us with a handsome plan, which I liked but which seemed quite impossible to execute. He had placed the vegetables on the southwest side of the house for sun and proximity to the kitchen: a sound enough concept, but that particular plot of land was literally on top of a rock quarry.

It was Lygia and her friends who overcame the obstacles of cost and labor when they began clearing rocks for the vegetable garden. Then we brought in a few truckloads of redwood mulch. This, along with our own piles of horse manure, compost heaps, and rotted oak leaves, which Donn and I shoveled from the ditch at the edge of the long driveway, made a good base with which to begin our garden. Moving all these piles and working them into the soil was not a simple job. Although each of the older children took his or her turn at the wheelbarrow, digging, or turning soil, we barely made a dent. When my friend Maggie heard we were preparing the whole area by hand, she sent her son down in a big van with their small tractor inside. That was friendship, pure and simple. With so much goodwill, and so much practical help, the garden had to be a success.

Those first few summers after the vegetable garden was planted, dinner hour came around later and later. In midsummer, the last ray of light wouldn't disappear until 9:15, at which time I would finally surrender and head back to the house. While I was becoming a better gardener, in self-defense Donn was becoming a better cook.

I had found that a garden laid out with harmony and rhythm and a variety of plant combinations added a whole new dimension to growing vegetables. It became a thing of beauty and a source of surprise. Every day felt like Christmas. I could hardly wait to run outside in the early light to see what the plants had done. Work truly became play, as I began weeding, watering, and clipping in the fresh cool air.

THE PLEASURES OF PLANTING

I adore every single part of gardening. Unlike kitchen cleanup, the garden cleanup chores of weeding and raking are ones that I actually enjoy. I can't muster much enthusiasm for a sponge, no matter how beautiful or practical it might be. But garden

tools—now, that's a different story. It makes a tremendous difference how a trowel, shovel, or clippers feel in your hand. I especially like the way tools feel when they've been used for a long while; the soft, satiny feel of wood that's been worn down by daily contact with the gardener's hand. I have an antique wooden rake that I regularly use and cherish along with a trowel my son Cyril made me in wood shop, one that has a strong metal blade and a wooden handle crafted just for my hand. Thanks to Smith & Hawken and a handful of other companies, you can now buy wonderful English tools here in America. I give one of their beautiful, pewter-like trowels to every young bride and groom I know. I hope the couple will have a garden one day, of course—but even if they don't, the trowel makes a perfectly fine flour or sugar scoop.

When all elements used in gardening are of natural materials, every stage of cultivating is an aesthetic pleasure. I use redwood stakes and natural twine to lay out the garden, wooden roof shingles to protect new plants from too much sun, small branches from pruned tree limbs for staking, and hand-split grapevine stakes for trellising.

Growing vegetables provides pleasure to all the senses. Taste, of course, is first and foremost, but smell, texture, and sound are important. However, I must confess to being most seduced by the sight of vegetables; after all, they are the most colorful part of the meal.

Perhaps it has to do with being raised in the city—I don't know—but seeing vegetables growing as ornaments in the garden is still a sight I don't take for granted. There's an intangible pleasure, a delight to seeing something we are accustomed to eating dotting the greenery like ornaments throughout the garden. Think about light filtering through translucent green lettuce leaves, or jewel-like purple eggplant hanging among unusually shaped gray-green leaves, or shiny orange peppers gleaming out from bright green leaves.

Besides companion planting for pest control and growth, think about planting for contrasts of color and texture and size. Vegetables can make a more spectacular border than flowers, if attention is paid to texture, rhythm, form, and color. Instead of putting curly parsley next to peas, beans, or peppers, try it next to broad-leaf escarole. Greens that go toward the reddish (red leaf chard) or purple (purple cabbage) also look wonderful next to light greens. One combination I've found particularly pleasing is large-leaf gray-green cabbage next to tall, two-year-old purple salvia.

DONN'S LAYERED VEGETABLES

Yellow zucchini are easy to grow, beautiful as a centerpiece, fun for children to pick, and most tasty in Donn's triple-layer treat.

1 teaspoon olive oil
2 cloves garlic, crushed
2 large sweet onions, sliced ½ inch thick
1 slightly overgrown zucchini or summer squash,
sliced ½ inch thick
2 large tomatoes, sliced ½ inch thick
Dried oregano
Cheddar, Jack, or Italian Fontina cheese

In a large skillet, heat olive oil and sauté garlic until tender. Layer bottom of the pan with slices of onion. On top of onions, place a layer of sliced squash. Compose the top layer of slices of tomatoes and a large handful of crushed dried oregano, or two handfuls of fresh oregano and some freshly ground pepper.

Turn heat to medium low, cover, and cook until fork-tender—about 20 minutes. Then sprinkle with grated cheese to taste. Put lid back on skillet until cheese is melted.

Purple Turnip Soup

After my vegetable centerpieces have had their moment onstage, I change their sculptured form to an edible one. And whenever I have a large number of vegetables, I think soup. Although I find most people's mouths don't water when I mention turnips, everybody adores this soup. It's very simple and straightforward. No measurements are necessary. Use your own taste buds to guide you with quantities. This same formula works for almost any vegetable. It's great for celery or carrots. To carrot soup, I sometimes add a little curry powder and top with toasted sesame seeds.

Fresh purple turnips (2 to 3 per serving)
Weak chicken stock
(½ chicken stock and ½ turnip water),
enough to thin soup to the desired consistency
Onions
Shallots
Garlic
Butter
Cream (optional)
Parsley, chopped
Slivers of chives

Boil turnips with skins until fork-tender. Drain, reserving water, and peel. Meanwhile, simmer the chicken stock in another pot. Sauté onions, shallots, and garlic in butter until golden. Toss onion mixture and turnips into blender, add chicken stock to reach desired consistency, and puree. Return mixture to saucepan and heat until hot.

You can add a little cream at this stage if you like, but it's not necessary. Garnish with chopped parsley or chives and serve hot.

Root vegetables are ideal for underwater bouquets.

Enjoy turnips as a centerpiece before you make your soup.

PULLING WEEDS AND PARENTING

Over the years, I've come to the conclusion that raising gardens and rearing children have many parallels. In the garden the task is much simpler. It's much easier to see what needs to be done, and the response is usually immediate. Vegetables are remarkably sanguine about not "talking back." Perhaps you remember the song from *The Fantasticks,* "Plant a Radish."

> *Plant a turnip, get a turnip, Maybe you'll get two.*
> *That's why I love vegetables,*
> *You know that they'll come thru!*
> *They're dependable! They're befriendable!*
> *They're the best pal a parent's ever known.*
> *While with children, It's bewilderin'*
> *You don't know until the seed is nearly grown*
> *Just what you've sown.*

To that, I say, "Amen."

PACING THE VEGETABLES

Each vegetable, like each human being, has an individual life cycle and distinctive characteristics. Some vegetables are delicious when picked young; others are tasteless and would serve better as a centerpiece, replanted in a box as a miniature vegetable garden. Very few gardeners allow their vegetables to go beyond the "perfect to pick" stage, especially with the recent craze for baby vegetables. Unfortunately, "perfect picking" can prematurely end an unfolding drama. Certain vegetables take on a dramatic quality when they're allowed to develop to a giant size. Take the pattypan, or scallop, squash—an ordinary little squash. Sometimes something that we are accustomed to seeing small takes on a different character when it bulges to a new dimension. It makes us feel we've opened Alice's secret door. It is curious how largeness anywhere creates an illusion of power.

Other vegetables exhibit interesting characteristics when allowed to mature all the way to the seed stage. Kale and cabbages, especially the purple varieties, have the most beautiful tall stalks, with delicate yellow flowers coming right up out of the round, solid base. Other examples of full-cycle beauty are artichokes, onions, leeks, and broccoli. I particularly like bronze-leafed Romaine Rouge d'Hiver and Cuore Pieno escarole.

Contained in a one-foot-square wooden box are brussels sprouts looking like cabbages; florets of cauliflower acting as cauliflower heads; radishes as beets; and an assortment of other baby vegetables and flowers, all planted in straight rows.

I'm sure that if Keats had seen this cabbage he would have written a sonnet about it. It seems almost sacrilegious to consider eating this beauty. Placing vegetables throughout the house emphasizes their importance, elevating them to a new status. Most often, these magnificent overgrown flowers—which bear little resemblance to the tight round heads of cabbage seen in the produce department—are found on our large coffee table in the living room. As long as they are in a shallow base of water, they are happy anywhere, but they particularly love the moisture of a bathroom.

Before they get too tall, one plant standing alone as an arrangement is stunning. Afterward, several on the table form a nice miniature lettuce forest.

THE ART OF VEGETABLES

Throughout history, painters have tried to capture the shapes, colors, and textures of vegetables and fruits. Think about a Cézanne still life and remember the eloquent statement of the simply grouped vegetables and fruits. The painting is art, of course, but as I see it, the vegetables, fruits, and flowers are themselves works of art.

If I were teaching studio art, I think, vegetables would be excellent candidates for teaching scale, form, texture, and proportion. Somehow all vegetables seem perfectly proportioned—the long-rooted carrot with its tall, lacy, multiple green stems, the smooth white leek with its sleek green top making one continuous line from tip to root, and the magnificent red-leaf chard with brilliant thick red veins and huge green leaves.

When it comes to textures, who can imagine a greater variation of surfaces than paper-smooth onion skin, prickly artichoke thistles, curly parsley, and bumpy cucumber? As for forms—I can't think of any other plants (except for underwater ones) that offer more strange and unusual shapes than vegetables, from the

Large purple kohlrabi always reminds me of martians with antennae all over their bodies.

JON-MARK'S SUMMER SALAD

*Serve a cauliflower soup followed by this beautiful salad, a
refreshing and colorful dish that can be served as an appetizer.
With the addition of shrimp or lobster, it's great for lunch or
supper when served with a rosemary brioche or French bread.*

*English or Armenian cucumber,
sliced, with skin scored but unpeeled
Honeydew melon
Mangoes
Avocados
Lime juice
Jalapeño chilies, finely chopped
Lobster claw, cooked*

*Arrange cucumber slices
in a fan pattern on plate.
Cut melon, mangoes, and
avocados in bite-size pieces,
toss at once with lime juice,
add chilies, and pile in the*
*center of the plate. The fruits
can be sliced instead of cut
and arranged by color to
make a pleasing pattern. Add
a large lobster claw on the
side of the plate.*

undulating forms of peppers, chayotes, gingerroot, and garlic to the miniature trees of the broccoli forest.

Originally, vegetables gave artists the means to paint, by providing pigment from their dyes. Still today, in order to accurately describe a color, we often use names of fruits or vegetables—lime green, beet red, lemon yellow, orange, or even that retail fashion favorite, aubergine.

So you see, vegetables are a work of art; now let's use them that way!

I see no reason that something as magnificent as a perfectly shaped pumpkin should be held prisoner in the kitchen. It looks splendid on the coffee table in the living room or on a pine bench in the guest room. Of course, I haven't forgotten that the primary purpose of the vegetable is to nourish the body. But vegetables can nourish the eye and the soul as well. I often have heads of unusual lettuces in bowls in the living room, pumpkins on the mantel, and a large glass bowl with only three perfect, huge red pomegranates or one or two gigantic cardoon leaves (five feet tall, eighteen inches across) on a low table.

VEGETABLE CENTERPIECES

Vegetables are a natural for a centerpiece. Vegetables either in the market or in the garden make their own suggestions, provide their own

DANNY KAYE ONCE BET HE COULD GIVE ME
A VEGETABLE I COULDN'T MAKE INTO A CENTERPIECE.
"TRY THIS DUMB POTATO," HE SAID. "THERE *ARE*
NO DUMB POTATOES," I ANSWERED, AND PROCEEDED
TO SELECT THE WEIRDEST YAMS I COULD AND
STOOD THEM UP IN A SHALLOW BRONZE CONTAINER.

CARISSA'S VEGETARIAN SAUCE

It is interesting that when children are young, they complain about vegetables; when they grow up, they become vegetarians. Carissa now makes the most marvelous and colorful vegetable dishes. I serve this as a first course without the pasta, adding only a little salt and pepper. Prawns can also be sautéed with the vegetables.

SAUCE
4 to 6 small red beets, quartered
2 to 4 carrots, cut into chunks
1 tablespoon tamari
1 tablespoon oregano
½ teaspoon paprika

VEGETABLES
1 tablespoon sesame oil
1 onion, quartered
1 carrot, sliced lengthwise
1 bell pepper, sliced lengthwise
1 yellow crookneck squash, cut into long thin pieces
½ cup sliced olives
1 cup fresh peas

For the sauce, boil beets and carrots in enough water to cover until soft. Blend in food processor or blender with most of the cooking water, tamari, oregano, and paprika. (Sauce should be thick and smooth, not watery.) Set aside.

For the vegetables, heat sesame oil in a sauté pan and sauté onion and carrot until

cooked. Add bell pepper and squash and cook lightly, 5 to 10 minutes, stirring constantly over medium high heat. At last minute, add olives and peas.

Serve sauce over pasta and top with vegetables.

Two ways to get your audience to pay more attention to vegetables— magnify them, or serve them in Carissa's Vegetarian Sauce. Both their chartreuse color and their shape make chayotes candidates for a still life with a purple pepper and fava beans.

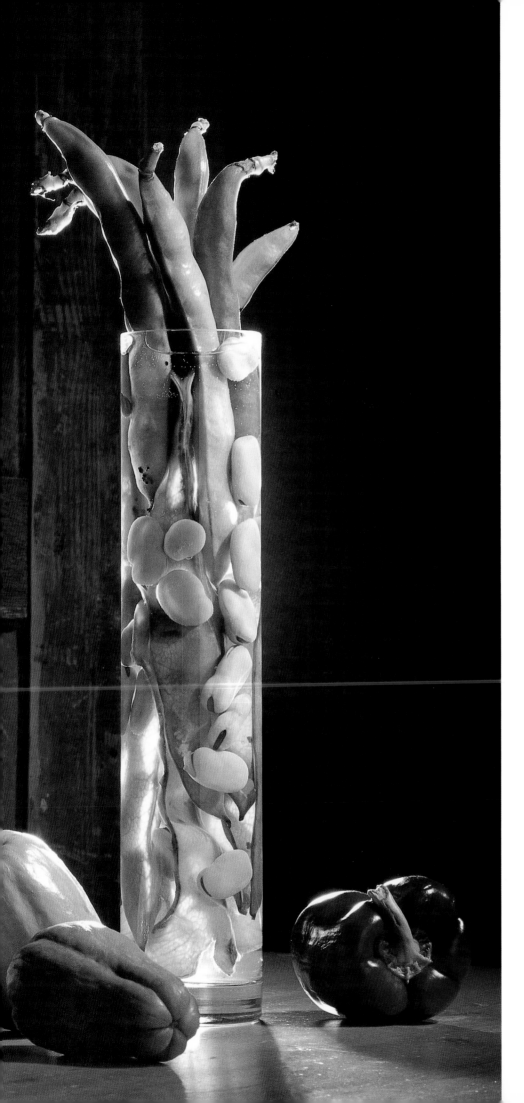

inspiration. Or I can decide what kind of mood I want to set for the evening—one of grandeur, elegance, sophistication, simplicity, or humor. There's no one correct way of using any particular vegetable. When a vegetable is not seen as a food object but as a form, new ideas for its use occur.

Some of the large events I design require many assistants. For me, one of the most enjoyable parts of planning these galas is seeing what new concepts develop. I've learned it's not just those we label "artistic" who come up with new ideas. In fact, very often I find it's the so-called inartistic person who arrives at the most original, bizarre, outrageous idea. It takes only freedom of thought.

While there certainly aren't any rules, I have developed a few prejudices. After working—or, rather, playing—with vegetables for many years, I find the less I do the more the beauty of the vegetables comes through. Two things are necessary—choosing an exceptional vegetable (which does not necessarily mean perfect) and placing it where it feels "right." There's really no formula for this. Your eye and instinct will tell you, if you allow yourself the privilege of time to play. One word of caution: if you're planning a table for the evening, think about what lights you'll use. Sometimes vegetables that look splendid and alive with color during the day can go dead and look washed-out at night. Experiment with different kinds of light.

Vegetables take on a new importance if they are not enclosed in a container or basket. There is nothing lovelier than an enormous head of cabbage by itself with all its outer leaves unfurled in welcome. It's like a giant rose in the middle of your table. Guests are always intrigued. Huge heads of green leaf lettuce are spectacular, too. While they need to be kept in water, if you use a shallow glass bowl the container can be completely hidden by the outer leaves. Napa cabbage also works very well. If you pull back some of the leaves, a form more like a giant, light-green flower appears. It's a curiosity because we're not accustomed to seeing flowers that size or color.

Those leafy vegetables mentioned above might be thought of as soft sculpture. The more usual sculptural approach, however, is to display items with hard edges and defined contours. Gourds and pumpkins of all sizes, shapes, and colors are natural sculptures, for instance. A line of eight perfectly round, yellow-gold winter squash, evenly spaced down the center of a rectangular table, is also striking. This idea can be carried a step further by varying the size. Different vegetables of the same color, such as a couple of large white pumpkins, some white eggplants, white onions, and a few little white gourds, create another kind of rhythm.

Many pieces of one vegetable, all the same size, color, and shape, displayed en masse provide a compelling centerpiece. There are many ways of doing this, and certain vegetables lend themselves to certain

It's always nice when you can provoke a laugh or at least get a smile from your guests. Celery stacked as Lincoln logs and broccoli as a miniature forest helps do this.

patterns. Mounds of artichokes, swirls of small Japanese eggplants, fans of Chinese bitter melon, pyramids of potatoes, flat diamonds of white onions, all take on characteristics of their own. Even bunches of tiny radishes, collected into an enormous cluster, are enchanting. Asparagus standing in a huge circle, upright in the middle of a table, is commanding, because how it manages to stay up is a bit of a puzzle. At an American Institute of Wine and Foods dinner, one of James Beard's favorite centerpieces was a bunch of leeks tied together with their roots reaching into the air. But these are just examples, not rules, not "recipes." Choose a vegetable that interests you and see what forms develop. No vegetable is too ordinary when presented with a sense of importance and style.

EDIBLE CENTERPIECES

The edible centerpiece is a cooking host's or hostess's dream. It can work for a table of four or a crowd of a thousand. While it takes a little time to prepare, depending on how elaborate you get, you can relax once it is on the table, as the food and the decoration are one. Here's one helpful hint: be sure you have more food than can be completely consumed at that meal, or your centerpiece will look depleted and messy.

Begin composing your edible centerpiece on a lazy Susan covered with cabbage leaves, or choose a

large, shallow basket so that the beautiful vegetables and whatever else you'll be serving will show well.

It is important to choose vegetables that will not wilt. If you include carrots, it is better to remove their delicate tops, leaving only a short green stem. Radishes with tops need to be conditioned (washed well, then sealed in a plastic bag and refrigerated for several hours) before using. Add a few large vegetables for scale, such as cabbage, eggplant, or cauliflower, that will remain fresh-looking throughout the meal.

Now, how to find all this grand and glorious fodder for your tablescapes? The best solution, of course, is to grow your own. Almost any sunny plot can become a garden if the soil is prepared and you give irrigation some thought. Many vegetables do well in small areas, even in containers. Plant a few extra vegetables, knowing that they are to be your ornamental bouquet as well as part of your edible garden.

Of course, vegetable bouquets are not the sole province of the vegetable gardener. Anyone can go to a supermarket or farmer's market these days and find beautiful fresh vegetables that will make magnificent centerpieces. When selecting vegetables for their aesthetic qualities, search out the unusual—different shapes or colors and textures. Then buy a large enough quantity to make a dramatic arrangement. Even if you end up buying twelve pounds of golden peppers, it will be less expensive than flowers and much more fun than a bouquet from the florist. And tomorrow, you can dine on golden pepper soup.

IT'S WORTH GROWING CUCUZZI SQUASH JUST
FOR THEIR EXQUISITE PAPER-THIN WHITE BLOSSOMS.
A MATURE SQUASH CAN BE TWO FEET LONG.

The old principles of design from nature still apply: *balance, rhythm, color, form, texture.* Grouping like vegetables together rather than spreading them throughout the basket is usually more pleasing. Atomize the produce with fresh water and store it in a cold room until ready to use. Except for more perishable items, these "arrangements" can be done in the morning.

There is no limit to what you can add to your centerpiece. Keep in mind it is also your table buffet, so choose vegetables that are good to eat as well as picturesque and durable. Some vegetables are more exciting when blanched, such as string beans, cauliflower, and asparagus. If you add a wonderful selection of breads and cheeses, suddenly you've got the entire meal in the middle of the table.

DRAMA FROM GARDEN TO TABLE

The garden teaches me that drama comes from being bold—six-foot-tall fennel, gigantic cardoon leaves, two-foot-long cucuzzi squash, mammoth pumpkin leaves, and the pumpkin itself— huge and rich in color. For James Beard's birthday dinner, we decided to let him know we knew—and appreciated—his taste as well as his books. Pigs' feet were among his favorite items, so—voilà!—they became our centerpiece, surrounded by baby red potatoes.

We also concocted tables with bread dough rising in a big copper pot, a big bowl of cookie dough, and ten-inch chocolate-chip cookies as star attractions. *Beard on Pasta* was represented by a large wooden fork and spoon stuck into a mountain of fresh pasta. One table was heaped with a mound of radishes, washed and oiled, shining under the lights. Another setting featured an artistic presentation of his brioche-and-onion sandwich in wild and uneven stacks. And then there was a commercial eighteen-inch whisk standing grandly on end, embedded in egg whites, with eggs in their shells nested all around. You'll have to ask Jim Dodge, author of *The American Baker*, how to make your egg whites hold together for several hours. When I think back to that dinner, I think about all the wonderful tables we did—and the tables we could have done.

If ever my courage with food, tables, or flowers fails, and I find myself drifting into conventional—or lazy—thinking, I remember N. C. Wyeth's counsel: "To go along with the drift of things is treason."

THE CUTTING GARDEN

*The earth laughs
in flowers.*

RALPH WALDO EMERSON

As wonderful as vegetables are, they don't smell like honeysuckle or lilac. And, as beautiful as the lavender blossom of the eggplant, or the golden trumpet flower of squash, there is nothing like a peony, a bearded iris, or a rose.

But it's not enough to admire flowers in the out-of-doors; I've come to believe that there's something absolutely instinctive in human beings that makes us want to pick a flower and bring it home. I've never seen a two-year-old in a meadow who didn't want to gather a fistful for the return trip.

There's been a lot written about human love encouraging plant growth, but I think it works both ways. Perhaps it's not just custom that dictates sending flowers to the sick. I'm convinced that plants give off an energy we can feel if we're receptive. When I walk into a room and glimpse a beautiful arrangement—flowers, vegetables, or greens—I get not only a sense of joy but a sense of energy as well. Beauty is a positive emotion. The energy I feel brings the title of Rilke's poem to mind: "At once on the winged energy of delight."

In the introduction to Katharine White's lovely collection *Onward and Upward in the Garden*, her husband, E. B. White, talks about watching her arrange flowers after a visit to her cutting garden.

Sometimes, as I sat quietly in my corner, watching her throw flowers at each other, it looked as though she were playing darts in an English pub. Whenever I could, I attended these flower-arranging sessions (they lasted only ten or fifteen minutes), because it was a little like going to a magic show. She seldom spoke during the show, seldom commented on the finished product. Once in a while she would make a pronouncement, sotto voce, "There! That's pretty." But there was always the hint of a question mark buried in there. "Is it? Is it pretty?" For Katharine, a room without a flower or plant was an empty shell.

For me, too. One day I realized there were no longer ten or more mouths to feed at every meal. So I decided it would be a nice idea to convert the last two sections of the vegetable garden into a cutting garden. Alas, there was one little detail of planning that I neglected. The last two sections of our vegetable garden happened to be located just below the terrace, overlooking the entire vista of the vineyard, winery, and valley below. This meant that every time I made a picking foray into the cutting garden, I left a bare spot right in plain view. I couldn't bear to look down and see that sad, empty space, so I picked gingerly, if at all.

Now, with two years under my trowel of working with my cutting garden, I am full of ideas about how to do it differently. Two things are important for a

garden to really function as a cutting garden. First of
all, it has to be very personal—planted with flowers,
shrubs, or vegetables that you like to use in your home.
Second, it needs to be hidden from easy view, so that
you can harvest away and not mind how the poor, bereft
garden looks.

DREAM THE IMPOSSIBLE DREAM

In my dream cutting
garden, I would begin with fields of a single color—of
cosmos, for example, just like the opening scene of *The
Color Purple*, where two young girls run through a mass
of waving lavender blooms. Then, I'd want a field of
pink lupine, a bank of tall delphiniums, an arbor of
sparrieshoop (a pink, single old-fashioned rose), a wall
of bearded iris in a rainbow of hues, and a section of
white Casablanca lilies. What else? Well, how about a
drift of orange, peach, and pink daylilies all together?
Then, an acre of or so of roses set off by themselves
with nepeta and lavender growing below. And, as long
as there's no limit on dreams, I'd add a few dozen
rhododendrons and azaleas for the winter and early
spring, and of course miles of Matilija poppies
everywhere. And, finally, I'd have an entire bank of
white, apple-blossom pink, and lavender petunias,
so wonderful as cut flowers.

I do have criteria besides aesthetics for my cuttables. Sometimes we forget that flowers have another purpose besides just giving us delight. They are the self-perpetuating part of the plant. Since I want to see the hillsides covered with wildflowers, I don't allow myself to pick *them*. I want things that can be cut without lessening or injuring the species. And, when cut, the plant or flower must last inside for a minimum of four or five days, and ten is better. Or, they must be so magnificent that one day's enjoyment is worth the effort. Giant magnolia blossoms and hibiscus fit into this category.

That's the ideal. Few of us have the space, time, money, or energy to plan such an idyllic cutting garden. But when I think about cutting gardens on any scale, I try to incorporate those principles. I want variety, "cutability," and durability, along with beauty.

CUTTING THE UNCUTTABLE

Like most gardeners, I envision an "ideal" cutting garden. In actuality, I end up cutting almost everything but poison oak.

Sometimes life and circumstances conspire to make the garden more useful as a cutting resource. I can't be a full-time gardener because planning special events, helping with public relations for the winery, running a household, and occasional duty as wife, mother, and grandmother intervene. Because of those other responsibilities, and despite the fact that I do have

*This perfect example
of the seven-minute
pick and put bouquet was
made by Sequoia,
age five.*

PICK AND PUT

If you're editing as you pick—or buy—the arranging is already done by the time you bring your flowers inside. Most of my arrangements are the seven-minute variety—pick and put. I have a lot of ways to pick and put, such as:

THE GARDEN SALAD
When you have the location in mind where the flowers will be placed, size and color are predetermined. Select almost whatever you bump into in that color and size.

MASSES OF ONE FLOWER
Often, with one flower, it's more interesting to have a variety of colors, such as blue and purple and pink—as in larkspur or delphinium.

MASSES OF ONE COLOR
One flower or several flowers of the same color.

FLORAL FUGUE
Each flower in its own container stands at a different level. Begin with one flower at one height, another at a different height, then another, ending with one floating low. I love to do this when peonies are in bloom, so that each glorious blossom is appreciated singly, not lost in a bouquet.

ONE SINGLE PERFECT FLOWER (USUALLY LARGE) OR ONE UNUSUAL BRANCH

ONE MASS OF DIFFERENT GREENS WITH ONE SINGLE LARGE FLOWER
Examples include a rhododendron blossom or three roses grouped together, preferably placed off center. The green will last for three weeks, and you can change the central flower when you change the water.

CLUMPS DUG UP WITH THEIR DIRT AND PUT IN A LOW CONTAINER
Examples are clumps of chives in bloom, clumps of Johnny-jump-ups, or a tuft of green grasses, barley, or wheat. Be careful to take enough dirt so that the plant does not fall apart. It will last several weeks inside. But before it gets too weak, return it to the earth.

When flowers are placed on the floor, we no longer see the blossoms in profile. We're forced to experience them in a new way. Face up, the intensity of color becomes more apparent.

Flowers do not require a special container. But if the container is special, then more care needs to be taken to choose flowers that are appropriate for it. Glass disappears, a fine characteristic, when you really want to see the flowers alone and unadorned. Since baskets are made from natural materials such as willow, reeds, natural vines, or even clay, they have an affinity with other living plant material. Of course, non-vases (such as pitchers, jars, tins, and mugs) are also great containers for flowers. If I were to give away advice, I would say buy one super-large container, about two feet wide and at least that tall. It needn't be terribly expensive—a huge basket or a crock from a hardware store is sufficient (something large enough to hold a five-gallon bucket). I haunt antique and junk shops looking for interesting, inexpensive, enormous containers.

When flowers are placed on the floor, we no longer see the blossoms in profile. We're forced to experience them in a new way. Face up, the intensity of color becomes more apparent.

Flowers do not require a special container. But if the container is special, then more care needs to be taken to choose flowers that are appropriate for it. Glass disappears, a fine characteristic, when you really want to see the flowers alone and unadorned. Since baskets are made from natural materials such as willow, reeds, natural vines, or even clay, they have an affinity with other living plant material. Of course, non-vases (such as pitchers, jars, tins, and mugs) are also great containers for flowers. If I were to give away advice, I would say buy one super-large container, about two feet wide and at least that tall. It needn't be terribly expensive—a huge basket or a crock from a hardware store is sufficient (something large enough to hold a five-gallon bucket). I haunt antique and junk shops looking for interesting, inexpensive, enormous containers.

some help in the garden, I often don't keep things as neatly clipped back as a truly conscientious gardener would. Thanks to that neglect, I have plenty of pruning to do, pruning that contributes to marvelous bouquets.

I confess I like a little wildness in a garden. I think it's artificial and boring to see the perfect edge of every path without anything overflowing. But I must admit, the growth along my garden paths goes a little too far from time to time, so that you almost need a scythe and a compass to find your way.

After they are well established, most trees or shrubs can use some pruning or shaping. I allow myself that privilege, but I am quite particular about who gets to wield the clippers or loppers in my garden. As I gather branches for an indoor bouquet, I try to look at the overall shape of the tree or bush, deciding what branch to eliminate in order to improve its health or appearance. As I walk or work around the garden, I'm constantly searching out the branches that could be separated to come inside. Then, when I need some branches, I usually have that reference tucked away in my head. I also spend some time "mentally pruning" when I'm on the telephone. Most of the rooms in our house have large windows, and I plant myself, phone tucked under chin, next to those windows, so that I can mentally file pruning information for future use.

GRAND-SCALE CUTTING

Orange trees can often stand some gentle shaping. When the pruned limbs with dangling fruit come inside, the feeling is more natural than that of a simple bowl of fruit.

On the mantel, large limbs that extend well beyond their container seem to float off in many directions, welcoming all who enter the room.

I used to think my bouquets were larger-than-life because I'm tall, and I like a certain element of eye-to-eye in interior design. But that can't be so. My associate, Alice Jones, a talented, wonderful lady who stands not quite five feet tall, loves to create big bouquets as well. In fact, I believe we don't even think of "bouquets" as such. Instead, we think about "bringing the outside in."

Treasures from the out-of-doors bring life into a room. When I walk into a room and see a large collection of branches, even if no one else is there, that room isn't empty or lonely. There's actually a presence that I feel. There's a connection with something living, and for a moment it's living inside, and I'm both the companion and the guardian.

Our *magnolia grandiflora* is one of my most treasured resources. Two qualities commend it: First, there's the intoxicating lemon perfume of the white blossoms. Then, there's the sheer spectacular size of the blooms. On the tree, the size looks proportionate, exactly right against those large dark, polished leaves. Once you bring the blossoms in, you see how enormous they really are—often ten or twelve inches across. The size doesn't make them forbidding; they're not harsh or spiky like a bird-of-paradise or a giant protea. Even without blossoms, bring the magnolia branches in. The size and sheen of the leaves are wonderful.

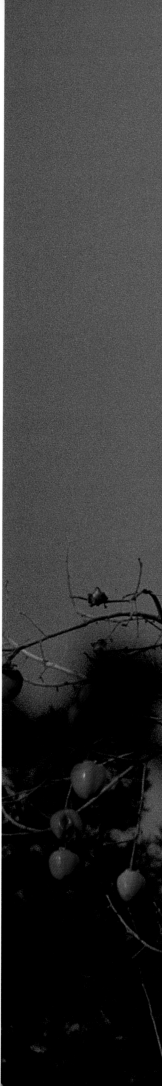

DONN'S WONDERFUL WAFFLES

These Hachiya persimmons are a great topping for Donn's Wonderful Waffles. Both James Beard and Marion Cunningham asked Donn for his recipe. Like most artists, he keeps experimenting. This version—made in a Belgian waffle maker— is the latest, and the best so far.

3 extra-large eggs, separated

1 cup sour cream

1 cup all-purpose flour

1 teaspoon baking soda

3 cups buttermilk

5 tablespoons melted butter

Assorted toppings, such as Vermont maple syrup, marionberry syrup and sliced fresh peaches, or chunks of ripe Hachiya persimmon

Combine egg yolks and sour cream. Add flour and baking soda. Stir in buttermilk, one cup at a time, and melted butter, combining thoroughly.

Beat egg whites until soft peaks form, and fold into batter. Bake in a Belgian, or other, waffle maker until golden and crisp.

*The refreshing lemon
scent and velvety softness
of the magnolia
flowers invite closeness.
I like to put one
perfect blossom next to the
bed of a guest or
float several in a pond—
or a bathtub.
For special occasions,
I've floated hundreds in a
swimming pool.*

With glycerine in the water, the leaves will stay pliable as they turn a warm, tawny brown. A single interestingly shaped magnolia branch can make a magnificent arrangement all by itself.

THE BLESSINGS OF SHRUBBERY

Shrubs are absolutely indispensable in our garden. They provide a variety of textures and are a terrific camouflage for our less than architecturally splendid house. I keep some shrubs in five- and fifteen-gallon cans just to have them on hand whenever I need them for portable drama or backdrops. As cutting plants they are equally indispensable.

The usual suspects are great—camellias, forsythia, and lilac. But I also enjoy cutting very long branches of white spirea, pale pink weigela, greenish-white blossoms of *Viburnum opulus*, eight-to-ten-foot branches of genista, short branches of daphne, hydrangeas, raphiolepis, peonies, and philadelphus. The miniature leaves of nandina add a lovely lacy texture to almost any arrangement. Rhododendrons and azaleas can last up to three weeks as cut branches.

Natal plum (*Carissa grandiflora*) is a pleasure indoors, with its shiny green foliage and white, sweet-smelling blossoms. It's one of my favorite shrubs, which is why our daughter Carissa carries the name she does.

THE CUTTER'S EYE

Flower arranging, like cooking and setting a table, reveals a person's character and style. In both cooking and flower arranging, I'm pretty messy. But I'm fast—I've had to be. I go for impact; that's why I like big-scale arrangements (I mean floor-to-ceiling) and small, dramatic ones—or something totally outrageous no one has thought of.

Flower arranging, like other art forms, reflects the culture and the times. Today's flower arrangements are more casual; there's a greater freedom of expression —few restrictions. I like arrangements that don't look arranged or contrived.

Placement need not be just on the center of the table. Often it is more interesting, even on a long dining table, not to have flowers in the center but to have them at one end, or to place a large bouquet at one end and a smaller bouquet or group at the other. But the flowers do not even need to be on a table. They can be above eye level, on a high mantel or bookshelf, or way below eye level, on the floor.

They don't even have to be *on* anything. They can hang on a door, from a ceiling, around the neck of either a person or a bottle. They can be pressed flat to send in a letter. They can be floated in a bathtub, a swimming pool, a hot tub, or a toilet bowl, or used to tie a present or crown a head. A wonderful welcome for a special guest is to cover a path with rose petals.

Everything from tall, sturdy corn to delicate lace-cap hydrangeas can be enjoyed indoors. Many people are afraid to cut hydrangeas; they're used to seeing them get the droops. Avoid this by cutting in the morning and submerging them, head and all, in warm water. They can also be resurrected by recutting and resubmerging. Corn can be treated as a regular cut flower. If cut in the fall, both will dry well and last for months.

When buckets of roses are set on the floor, you appreciate the saturation of color more because you're looking directly into their faces, not distracted by the contour. Placing an extra-large bouquet in a small room with few or no windows can add a window of greenery and make a dreary little room feel like a garden.

Last year, when we floated four thousand roses in a swimming pool as a spectacular display for a wedding, I became a rose near-expert in self-defense. All it took was lots of roses, clear fishing line, weights painted to match the bottom of the pool, and plenty of hand-tying and we had one of the most memorable wedding sights in the Napa Valley. Selected colors from my garden and two spectacular rose gardens, those belonging to Dede Wilsey and Susan Robbins, added greatly to the hothouse roses. At the end of the festivities, the groom's friends helped themselves to some of the roses, tied them to the car, and sent the young lovers off in a cloud of petals and fragrance. What a beginning to their life together!

While a swimming pool is an ideal "giant" container, baskets and glass bowls can work just as well. If the containers show and are ugly you can always tie burlap, canvas, or colorful tablecloths or bedspreads around them, or around a five-gallon bucket filled with branches, a tree, or flowers. Small containers can, of course, be covered with moss, grasses, or leaves.

*When chives are
in full bloom, I like to
borrow the whole
clump from the garden for
my table. When they
finish flowering, I replant
them in their original spot.*

*I enjoy the close
color harmonies that we
often find in a single
flower. The subtle changes
of hue in the iris, from
yellow to lavender to pale
rust, can inspire
delightful combinations
of similar colors
throughout the house.*

217

MAGIC FORMULA FOR LASTING FLOWERS

When florists say their flowers have been conditioned, it simply means they have been freshly cut and put in deep water until they have soaked up all the water they can.

Some flowers need more care than others, but almost no plant can resist this kind treatment.

Cut early in the morning, using a sharp knife or clippers. Cut stem on a slant and make a slit up each stem, at least three inches if the stem is woody. Put directly into a deep bucket of warm water for several hours. In case of a wilt, recut and repeat the same method. Some plants need time to revive—sages, most herbs, artemisias. Store the plants in a cool, dark area to retard opening.

Plants with milky stems— such as poinsettias, euphorbias, oriental and Iceland poppies, and ranunculus—don't respond well to this treatment. Their stems need to be sealed with a flame or boiling water immediately after cutting. Other plants respond better if they're pampered just a little by having the warm-water bucket brought to them. Roses and Matilija poppies are two such delicate creatures. Transvaal (gerbera) daisies seem to prefer ice water up to their necks.

SUNDAY ARRANGEMENTS, OR A LITTLE
MORE TIME ON MY HANDS

Most of my arrangements are the seven-minute variety—pick and put. But when I do have time to *arrange* flowers, I like to explore unusual combinations. Recently I've been enjoying arranging flowers as if they were growing— sometimes all in one container, sometimes each flower in a separate container. Redwood suckers are marvelous to cut and stick into dirt as if growing, and they last several weeks. If the container is very low (which is usually the best look for this sort of arrangement), it's necessary to use pin frogs to make the redwood branches stand up. This can also be done in water. Of course, bulb flowers with straight stems are natural for this, but oriental poppies look great this way, too. Bearded iris or ranunculus look wonderful standing straight up in a shallow container, sometimes with large spaces between the flowers, looking as if they were growing in the earth. One of the prettiest and simplest examples of this idea I've seen was one February in the Napa Valley at the home of Barbara Eisele, of the Eisele Vineyard. Barbara set a stunning table using a pale yellow tablecloth with champagne flutes lined up along the center of the table, each of which held a single stem of a different height of mustard. So simple, so perfect, and just a weed.

I like my guests to have a salutation even before I greet them, so I make welcome swags to put on the front door. I don't wait for Christmas to hand out a wreath.

221

Why do people think wreaths have to be round? If you must make a form, why not a rectangle or triangle? I prefer to simply make a long bunch (or swag) of colorful weeds, flowers, vegetables, or fruit.

On the opposite side of the grand scale, which is usually my great passion, is the oriental tradition of restraint. While I love huge, I also enjoy using one or two great flowers with a twig or some leaves.

THINKING OF COLOR

If I have a favorite color, I guess it's purple. It was here on Pritchard Hill before we came, in the distant hills and in the late-evening sky. And then, I kept planting more and more purple— eggplants, kohlrabi, purple onions and purply bronze sage, hydrangeas, purple penstemon, *Salvia superba 'purpurea,'* buddleia, and lavender. For me, purple is a neutral color, working well with so many different hues that it complements the entire color wheel in different ways.

But you probably have your own favorite. That's what counts. I can't imagine a day or a room without something from outside to remind us of what's just beyond the window or door. As I've written this book—indoors, regrettably, most of the time—the sight of one perfect Matilija poppy or a few spectacular buckeye branches has kept me going, with pleasure— and passion.

THE VOLUNTEER GARDEN

I love volunteers—in any field! Like most of us, always having more work than time, I'm most grateful

for volunteers whenever and wherever they appear. I even love the root of the word itself, from the Latin

voluntas, meaning will or wish. Working at the Los Angeles County Museum of Modern Art for ten years

as a docent, with other docent volunteers, gave me a great respect for people who give freely of their time

and energy. One of the things I learned from that experience was that volunteers are generally enthusiastic

and joyful. They work because they want to. They may or may not have had the proper training for the job,

but they cheerfully locate and relocate themselves to best use their skills and talents. And so it is with

our garden volunteers—plants reseeding themselves wherever they choose. Somehow they, like people,

seem happier when they have determined where they want to be. They are often stronger than plants we

deliberately plant; and if they appear in the middle of a path they don't mind being relocated, as long as

it's done with some care. Slowly, over the years, our cultivated garden has become freer, wilder, and more

imaginative. (I would never have dared place some plants where they volunteered to grow—trees four inches

from the house, for example.) Sometimes it seems to me the best gardening is like good improvisational

theater or jazz—the more talented the players, the more interesting the improvisation. However, not every musician or plant, no matter how talented, can perform this way. And sometimes totally untrained people can improvise amazingly. Plants we never think of as "volunteers" suddenly appear. Most of the plants that have volunteered in our garden I originally introduced by planting a seed or a cutting. However, some, such as the four-o'clocks, I never planted, and since our neighbors are miles away, there must have been some triathlon birds visiting here. Perhaps my cultivated garden understands that my heart belongs to the wilds, and welcomes volunteers as guests, not intruders. While I appreciate the science of gardening, my early education in art has led me to approach our garden as an art form, full of mysteries and surprises. I enjoy the inventiveness that volunteerism presents to me—plant placement and cultivation I might never have envisioned. And so the wild garden and my cultivated garden have mingled as friends—perhaps unpredictably, but continually giving delight. That is, in fact, the property of gardening I value most. It is a generous art and science. If you provide something—care, imagination, food, water—the garden will give back. Though I used to think of these "surprise appearances" as volunteers, I now see that the entire art of gardening is a volunteer exchange, a gift of work given freely and lovingly, and compensated in generous measure.

THE ARTICHOKE ARCH

Is this my artichoke or yours?

COLUMBINE TO PIERROT,
ARIA DA CAPO,
EDNA ST. VINCENT MILLAY

When I first planted eight little globe artichokes (*Cynara scolymus*) in a curve bordering the vegetable garden, I had no idea what magic would explode a few years later all over the garden. When left to fully develop, the artichoke is an ever-changing artform. It is also a surprisingly accurate mirror for human nature and for the stages of growth we all go through—some graceful, some not, but all interesting and all essential.

In the early spring, silvery-green leaves begin to appear. Soon the artichoke takes shape as a small handsome bush. This is the way most people know the artichoke—a compact, beautiful gray-green plant with enormous, jagged leaves bearing an edible bud, or "king head." The artichoke, interestingly enough, is one of the few vegetables we eat at the bud stage.

Perhaps because I've been fortunate (or challenged!) enough to raise sons, I confess that the sight of an artichoke always puts me in mind of little boys. If you leave a bud or two on your artichoke plant, and let it "go to seed divinely," you'll know what I mean.

First of all, the result of a little benign neglect is a wonderful surprise—a spectacular deep-purple-to-blue blossom. But, as with little boys becoming young men, you pay a price for that splendor.

There's a gawky stage, when suddenly the stem sprouts tall, absurdly out of proportion to the plant.

Most of the large leaves die. When that happens, I think back to my own boys as teenagers, sprouting in all directions. Man-like creatures shedding little-boy bodies and the last vestiges of puberty. There's bravado, thorny sarcasm, and the hint of a ruggedly handsome "something" about to burst forth. It's a matter of many deep breaths, endless patience, and trust. Somehow, it seems easier to trust and accept inevitable growth in plants than in children. But patience can be rewarded. You may awaken one fine morning and find the most magnificent surprise—a sturdy, free-thinking, handsome being—before you. Behind him, the dazzling purple plumes of a thistled artichoke have blossomed quite unexpectedly as well. Still, the surprises aren't over—with artichokes or young men.

After this spectacular show of color, the brilliant purple flower will begin to fade; no longer a show-stopper, only a rather brownish-lavender dry thistle. I sometimes think of it as a plant experiencing its very own mid-life crisis. It's tempting to pull out this strággly thistle, thinking the best is over. But patience! Wait for the final act! A golden glory is about to take place, as the artichoke creates exciting new beginnings as a stately gold blossom, freely releasing its seeds to the wind and birds. Then it starts all over again.

My own sons are still young, still full of the energy and color of youth. But I'm looking forward to their middle age, and to their own experiences of new color and new adventures.

GOING TO SEED DIVINELY

According to Greek mythology, a jealous goddess turned Cinara into a thistle. But Cinara had her revenge by bursting into a magnificent iridescent purple blossom. The black bumblebee, with its extra-long tongue, is one of the few bees that can extract nectar from the deep thistles.

Artichokes are hardly newcomers to horticulture. The Egyptians cultivated them as early as 600 B.C., and you can see artichokes used as decorative motifs in ancient frescoes. The Romans used the leaves in salad, and preserved them as well. In the fifteenth or sixteenth century, two varieties of the plant—globular and conical—were introduced in Europe, probably wending their way northward from Sicily. Artichokes enjoyed a brief period of scandal during Catherine de Médicis's time. Catherine fell in love with the prickly vegetables and ate them with gusto —in public! This despite the fact that they were considered a powerful aphrodisiac. The Spaniards first brought the artichoke to California. Today, California produces virtually all of America's artichoke crop.

In our garden, artichokes have been allowed to reseed themselves wherever they wish. We've been rewarded for our permissiveness; in the summer we now have the most dramatic display of ten-foot-tall, exotic purple flowers. Towering bouquets, arching overhead, stand like purple guardians throughout the garden.

I like that look so much I cut the giant stalks and bring them into the entrance hall to welcome guests. When I'm armed with sturdy gloves (to keep the spines away), I tie up a large swag of these brilliant purple thistles to create a note of welcome on the front door.

GOING TO SEED DIVINELY

According to Greek mythology, a jealous goddess turned Cinara into a thistle. But Cinara had her revenge by bursting into a magnificent iridescent purple blossom. The black bumblebee, with its extra-long tongue, is one of the few bees that can extract nectar from the deep thistles.

Artichokes are hardly newcomers to horticulture. The Egyptians cultivated them as early as 600 B.C., and you can see artichokes used as decorative motifs in ancient frescoes. The Romans used the leaves in salad, and preserved them as well. In the fifteenth or sixteenth century, two varieties of the plant—globular and conical—were introduced in Europe, probably wending their way northward from Sicily. Artichokes enjoyed a brief period of scandal during Catherine de Médicis's time. Catherine fell in love with the prickly vegetables and ate them with gusto —in public! This despite the fact that they were considered a powerful aphrodisiac. The Spaniards first brought the artichoke to California. Today, California produces virtually all of America's artichoke crop.

In our garden, artichokes have been allowed to reseed themselves wherever they wish. We've been rewarded for our permissiveness; in the summer we now have the most dramatic display of ten-foot-tall, exotic purple flowers. Towering bouquets, arching overhead, stand like purple guardians throughout the garden.

I like that look so much I cut the giant stalks and bring them into the entrance hall to welcome guests. When I'm armed with sturdy gloves (to keep the spines away), I tie up a large swag of these brilliant purple thistles to create a note of welcome on the front door.

ARTICHOKE SALAD

It is hard to beat the compelling power of the purple thistle, but it was the fruit, not the blossom, that ancient Greeks, Romans, and Egyptians served as a delicacy to the aristocracy. Donn favors the edible form, too.

Artichokes (1 per serving)
Fuji persimmons (1 per serving)
3 parts hazelnut oil
1 part balsamic vinegar
1 part rice vinegar
Salt and pepper to taste
Chopped roasted hazelnuts

Cook artichokes until tender. Drain, cool, and remove hearts. Cut hearts into ¼ inch round slices. Slice persimmons crosswise ¼ inch thick. Arrange slices on plate, alternating layers of persimmon and artichoke heart. Combine oil, vinegars, and salt and pepper and drizzle dressing over all. Sprinkle with chopped nuts.

I fill in with bunches of lavender, conveniently enough in bloom at the same time the artichokes turn purple and regal. Hung upside down, the artichokes tend to show the intricate form of their purple faces.

Dominic, six feet, three inches tall, has to stand on his toes to cut the artichoke blossoms. Hung on the front door under the covered porch, out of the sun, the blossoms will keep their deep purple color for weeks.

TO EVERY THING, THERE IS A SEASON

The iridescent purple flowers are almost enough of a reason to grow artichokes, but I love them in all their stages. There's nothing quite like the large, gray, fern-like leaves (three to five feet in length) to contrast color and texture in the garden. Whether used singly for an accent in a small courtyard or repeated at different intervals throughout a larger garden, they add a definite focal point and require almost no care—if you are not concerned with eating them. They are totally drought-resistant and fit perfectly into my favorite plant category—*Thrive on Neglect*.

But suppose you've got the taste of tender young leaves in your mouth, a mental picture of butter melting, or curry-spiked mayonnaise crying out for a dippable leaf. Well, then, you've got to be a kinder, more attentive gardener.

In order to form good, edible heads, the plants must be divided at least every three years. With a sharp knife, the offshoots are cut from the mother plant, taking a bit of the heel to hold the plant together. If this is done

in March, the new plants will produce heads in the fall.
New plants can, of course, be planted from seed, but
will take longer to form the vegetable. If you stagger
your planting, you can have artichokes to eat from
May through October.

Good soil, fog, and moderate temperatures
are ideal conditions for growing the best artichokes.
That's why Castroville (south of San Francisco, near
the ocean) is the artichoke capital of the world and
serves artichokes in thousands of ways. We, too, have
our own personal recipes. Alexa wraps an artichoke
heart in two slices of fried eggplant. Jon-Mark likes an
artichoke, grapefruit, and sun-dried tomato salad with a
dash of cayenne. When the heads first form is Donn's
favorite time to feast on artichokes. They're so small and
tender at this stage, you can eat the whole thing, choke
and all. The rest of the family enjoys a cheese soufflé
baked inside an artichoke, using the leaves as spoons for
the soufflé.

The cardoon, an artichoke look-alike that we
also grow, is prized for its stalk. To have really tender
stalks, it is necessary to blanch the plant while it is still
growing, to protect it from sunlight. Jean Troisgros
showed me how to tie up the leaves, then bind them
with straw or burlap. Then he cooked the cardoons for
us, using only the innermost ribs. (Unlike artichokes,
cardoons, with their slightly broader leaves and smaller
heads, have to be raised from seed.)

*E*qually dramatic as this large bouquet of leaves is a bowl with a single gigantic artichoke leaf. When cut early in the morning and immediately immersed in deep water, these leaves can last up to a week.

*T*he tall purple blossoms require the same care in picking, but even when their leaves get droopy, the stalks and flower heads are stately. Simply pick off leaves that look dead. Eventually, when the stems have taken up enough water, they slowly dry out and can be kept for months.

241

Before the plants form heads is the optimum time to cut cardoon and artichoke leaves to use indoors. One gigantic five-foot leaf is enough to make a striking arrangement by itself—two or three make a gorgeous bouquet. (Again, be sure you make your attack wearing heavy gloves. Artichokes and cardoons feature very spiny leaves—and when they have been allowed to revert to thistles, they get even pricklier.)

Both artichokes and cardoons require protection from frost by mulching with leaves or straw and heaping dirt around their stems. Last winter, I was worried we had lost all our artichoke plants when they were blackened by frost. But the roots survived, and when the cold subsided they pushed forth new green leaves.

There is something quite human and endearing about artichokes. In Fellini's wonderful film *La Strada*, the protagonist calls his sweetheart *Carciofo*, "little artichoke ." A little prickly, a little secretive, but filled with tender delights: that's his beloved and the funny, surprising, volunteering plant we call *Cynara scolymus*.

THE PUMPKIN PATCH

On the coast of Coromandel
Where the early pumpkins blow,
In the middle of the woods
Lived the Yonghy-Bonghy-Bò.

EDWARD LEAR

I don't know just where that coast of Coromandel is—nor, I suspect, does anyone else. However, I'd be happy to visit there, because I love the idea of a place that has "early pumpkins."

Every fall, when the dazzling orange, aqua, peach, white, and even blue pumpkins are maturing in our patch, I just can't wait for them to grow up and surprise me with size and shape.

Whether the garden-variety old orange pumpkins, growing stout and grand in a commercial field, or a single white pumpkin on a shiny black piano, I think pumpkins have a beautiful, sculptural quality and a kind of whimsy all their own. Because of their size and shape, pumpkins show off best when they're not trapped in a container but placed directly on a surface. If you treat them like pieces of sculpture, they fulfill that artistic vision. Just give them the space and importance they deserve and they will delight you for months as works of art. I have had some white ones that lasted a year. (One housekeeping caution: some varieties will last for months; others go soft on the bottom after only a month or two. Be sure to select a firm pumpkin and check periodically. If it starts to go bad, it will take the finish off your furniture.)

SEND ME A PUMPKIN

Pumpkins are really annual
vines, related to gourds, melons, and squash. If you're a
traveling gardener, you know that you can find gourds
almost all over the world—throughout the United
States, Europe, Mexico, China, Africa, and the Soviet
Union. They're prolific growers; the Pilgrims virtually
lived on pumpkins their first hard winter, a survival
diet they learned from the Indians. Perhaps you know
"The Pilgrim Song":

> *We have pumpkin at morning*
> *and pumpkin at noon.*
> *If it were not for pumpkin,*
> *we would be undoon.*

Pumpkins don't mean survival to me, but I
dearly love strolling through a pumpkin patch in
October. In Northern California, many of the
commercial growers center their activities near the coast
at Half Moon Bay. Thousands of people make a semi-
pilgrimage to the pumpkin patches, bundling up against
the brisk fall wind and walking through, stopping to
admire one enormous specimen and to chuckle at
another, lumpy and oddly shaped, looking for all the

world like a retired prizefighter. People make their
selections carefully, only after photographing their
children perched atop a giant pumpkin or clutching half
a dozen tiny white pumpkins to their parkaed chests.
They're destined for use as jack-o'-lanterns, of course,
but I always hope some of them stay intact, nature's
own sculpture, to adorn virtually any surface.

Most of all, I think I love the innate surprise of
the pumpkin. Early in the season, the lush growth and
bright orange trumpet flowers barely hint at the drama
that will follow. But, sure enough, right on schedule, as
Halloween creeps around the corner, the leaves die back
and the pumpkin surprises emerge.

One year I planted columns of corn, leaving
about seven feet between columns. Pumpkins were
planted around the base of the columns. Not only was
it a spectacular sight, but the corn gave the pumpkin
leaves enough shade that they didn't wilt.

It's hard to be serious or stuffy around a
pumpkin. Once, Macy's department store gave me an
assignment to "pumpkin-up" their china department.
I found 150 various-sized pumpkins I just had to have.
There was nothing to do but rent a pickup and drive it
from the pumpkin patch to Macy's loading dock.
Apparently, not many of their guest lecturers arrived
in such style; my appearance caused something of
a commotion.

ME FIRST; NO, ME!

Sometimes I simply line up pumpkins on the kitchen counter. Sitting there watching the hubbub in the kitchen, they remind me of children waiting for breakfast. Of course, the noise level is considerably lower. In my house, like the children, they simply appear, sometimes when and where you least expect them. I know I must have put them in one room or another, but it's always a surprise—and a delight—to see them.

Pumpkins truly are great volunteers. They show up on the compost heap, where rotted pumpkins or seeds have been deposited, in funny corners of the cutting garden, wherever we've plowed composted material back into the earth and in a few places where we haven't. Their splendid leaves, sometimes twelve inches across, provide wonderful contrast to the finer foliage of the flowers in my cutting garden—so wonderful, in fact, that I wish I could "art-direct" more of them into place. But that's the nature of volunteers; you have to take them where they show up.

Of course the pumpkins that "volunteer" their way onto my kitchen counter aren't long for the world in their original shape. If they sit there for a while, they turn into a soufflé or a spicy pumpkin soup. Once I served Jean Troisgros pumpkin soup in the pumpkin itself, a beautiful blue-green variety with pink stripes.

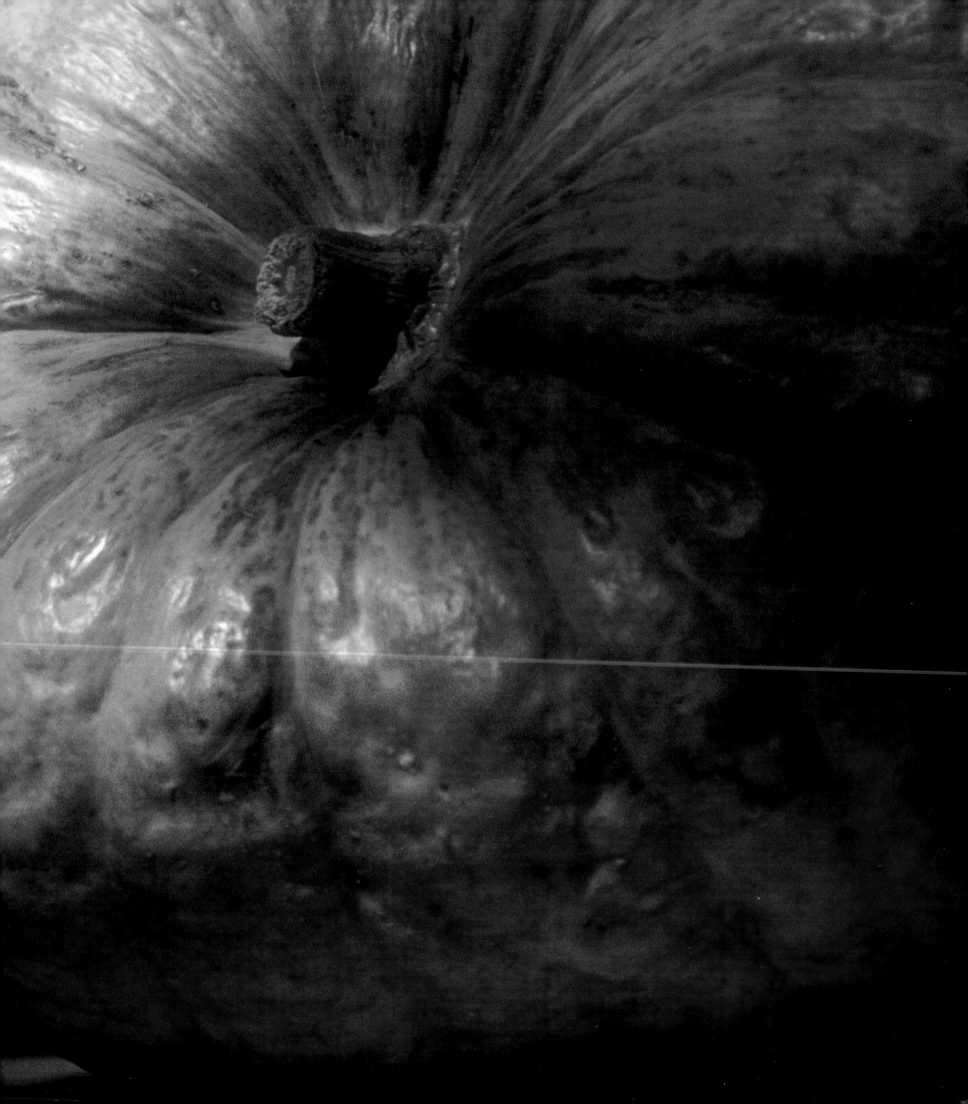

I don't know whether he was seduced by the soup or the container, but he set a small thrill going in my heart when he asked for the recipe.

A PATCH OF MANY COLORS

I'm a little fickle with pumpkins. My favorite used to be the enormous, smooth-skinned, pale peach variety. Then we grew the pure white ones, the celadon group, apricot beauties, and the mysterious-looking Queensland blue, a shiny, dark blue-green pumpkin. It's an eye-stopper when it's used in place of a bouquet.

Pumpkins are an irresistible theme for a party. At a luncheon in San Francisco at the beautiful L'Etoile restaurant, I lacquered a small legion of pumpkins. We painted them luminescent orange, apricot, peach, and pink. It produced a very elegant, sophisticated look. And a contrast, I might add, to a country luncheon where we used similar colors, but all *au naturel.*

At a special luncheon at San Francisco's L'Etoile restaurant, each table featured a different configuration of pumpkins lacquered to echo the colors in the painting on the wall above them. It's really quite easy to add a little glamor and sizzle to a pumpkin.

You can glaze the whole thing by applying several coats of paint and then a coat of lacquer. You can mix iridescent powdered gold, silver, platinum, copper, or pewter pigment with paint for a wonderful combination. Or, you can buy pastel colors and then apply a light coating of copper, silver, or gold.

When Dominic arrived home for Christmas one year, he said, "Mom, I love our Christmas tree." When I asked which one, he responded, "Any one you want. I might not have recognized them if I hadn't been reared in this family."

The original inspiration for the country party came from three grand-scale (ninety-five pounds each!), pale apricot, smooth-skinned pumpkins displayed at a cocktail party for Julia Child at the Culinary Academy in San Francisco. Two of these larger-than-life specimens squatted on a dark-brown lacquered bar, almost at eye level. One presided all alone at a table across the room. What a party that was! The guests couldn't stay away from the pumpkins, giving them pokes, smiles, even an outright laugh or two.

At the country luncheon, the pumpkins provided a perfect echo of the pumpkin-colored barns and the room where the party was given. To help things along, we painted paper lanterns in the same hues as the pumpkins, and hung them from the ceiling, creating the feeling of pumpkins floating all around the room. We did consider having a totally pumpkin menu, but cooler heads—and tummies—prevailed. Instead, we served a light saffron soup and a delicious smoked-salmon salad, and introduced the pumpkin for dessert—pumpkin cheesecake, pumpkin crème caramel, pumpkin bread pudding, and miniature pumpkin soufflés. I assure you, if someone had said "pumpkin" to a guest leaving the party, the guest would have had other word associations besides "pie" and "Halloween."

THE BEAUTIFIERS

Pumpkins are such accommodating additions to the garden. The plants grow so quickly they're great for a quick landscape cover-up against an old shed, fence, or garage. They're great fun for children, because the young gardeners see results—fast! They require heat and careful watering (try not to get the foliage wet), and they love manure. If you're interested in growing a giant-size specimen, strip off all but one vegetable from the vine when the pumpkins reach tennis-ball size. If you're growing for eating, rather than sculpture or carving, grow the smaller varieties with sweeter flesh—"small sugar pie," "Triple Treat," "Lady Godiva," "Sweet Meat," or "Tricky Jack" for the seeds. The last two varieties develop seeds without hulls, and are perfect to roast in the oven and salt for great snacks. Of course, you can also just see what appears and take your pumpkins as they come.

One of the most original plantings of pumpkins was done by my inventive five-year-old grandchild, Sequoia. Gathering a basket of the miniature sweet dumpling pumpkins, she "planted" them all in a line where newly prepared soil was dark and raked. It was an amazing as well as amusing sight, and even though we all knew better, they seemed to be growing neatly in a row.

INDIVIDUAL PUMPKIN SOUFFLÉS

This recipe is fun and easy when done in two stages. On the first day, I hollow the pumpkins out with a slotted spoon and make the pumpkin paste with the crème pâtissière. All I have to do the second day is assemble it.

8 pumpkins, about 3½ inches high by 4 inches wide
Additional pumpkin meat, cut into 2-inch chunks
¼ cup sugar

CRÈME PÂTISSIÈRE

6 eggs, separated, at room temperature
⅔ cup sugar
1 teaspoon vanilla
½ cup all-purpose flour
2 cups milk, scalded
Sugar
⅛ teaspoon freshly grated nutmeg
⅛ teaspoon cinnamon
¼ teaspoon cream of tartar

Cut tops off the pumpkins. Remove seeds and fibers. Scoop out the meat and reserve, leaving a cavity with 1-cup capacity and ¼- to ½-inch-thick walls. Invert pumpkins and dry on a rack overnight.

Weigh the pumpkin meat. Add enough additional meat to make 1 pound total. Transfer meat to a large, heavy saucepan, cover with water, and add ¼ cup sugar. Cook over low heat, swirling pan occasionally, until sugar dissolves. Increase heat and bring to a boil. Cook for 15 minutes, reduce heat, and cook until tender. Mash and continue cooking, stirring, until pumpkin is reduced to a thick paste, about 30 minutes. Cool to room temperature. Measure 1 cup to use in recipe. (Cover and refrigerate if making a day ahead.)

For crème pâtissière, beat egg yolks with sugar and vanilla in the bowl of an electric mixer until pale yellow and ribbons form. Mix in flour. Add hot milk in a thin stream, beating constantly. Pour into a heavy saucepan and stir over medium heat until mixture boils. Reduce heat and simmer 2 minutes, stirring constantly. Pour into a bowl, cool, cover, and refrigerate.

Preheat oven to 475 degrees. Generously sprinkle inside of each pumpkin with sugar. Combine 1 cup pumpkin puree, crème pâtissière, nutmeg, and cinnamon in a heavy saucepan over medium heat. Stir until lukewarm. Beat egg whites with cream of tartar until stiff but not dry. Fold a third of the whites into the pumpkin mixture. Gently fold in remaining whites. Fill pumpkins nearly to rims. Bake 10 minutes. Reduce oven temperature to 400 degrees and bake until soufflés are brown and puffed, about 10 minutes.

Serve immediately.

If you grow pumpkins in your garden, you truly are part of a long American tradition, dating to the Native Americans. Much of their diet depended on corn, pumpkins, and beans. Corn and pumpkins are very compatible companions in the garden. Just keep your pumpkins away from the potatoes—they don't work well together.

Every year, I peruse the seed catalogs, enjoying all the varieties of pumpkins. But somehow, much as I enjoy those I plant and nurture, none excites me quite as much as the "volunteers"—those surprises that pop up in the vegetable garden, in the compost heap, or that somehow, someday, just get themselves arranged on our terrace, marching like handsome smooth-skinned soldiers around the planters and up to the tables. I love their sizes, their shapes, and the wonderful thump they give back when you deliver a pat to their sides. In the fall, when they're so plentiful, I can't resist letting them into every nook and cranny of the house, and my family swears they hear me humming the pumpkin song under my breath. Well, who knows? Perhaps they do.

INDEPENDENT EDEN

There is nothing more deceptive than an obvious fact.

SHERLOCK HOLMES TO DR. WATSON

Here's the fact: gardening is hard work.

Well, yes—and no. It is hard work, as anyone who's spent a day weeding, digging, shoveling compost, and bending over to deadhead just one more plant knows. But, as the "volunteers" demonstrate again and again, sometimes it's no work at all. Sometimes, the most wonderful things happen in a garden—without the gardener's lifting a finger.

One of the joys that fall to the absentee gardener is to return to the garden, after being neglectful for some time, and see that—just like an orchestra playing away without a conductor—life continues in the garden. It is often amazing to me what a wonderful job the wind, the bees, the birds, and, with luck, the rain, can do in planting. Together, they are far more imaginative and daring than I, creating a kind of independent Eden.

A few years after we moved into "Motel 6," a small maple tree appeared just outside the game-room window. Literally just outside—it began growing just a few inches from the base of the house. Within two or three years, it had already begun to give much-needed shade in an otherwise sun-baked area. Today, it is forty feet tall, with branches reaching out and shading a third of the terrace and lowering the summer temperature in the kitchen and game room by ten degrees.

The ailanthus tree made its first appearance in front of our house, smack in the middle of the driveway, about twenty years ago. When I first saw this small tree appearing, I asked our local nurseryman what it was. He could hardly contain himself. "Get it out, get it out quickly, it will spread its seeds everywhere."

"Wonderful," I said. We were desperate for shade in our front entrance, and now we have about a dozen beautiful forty-foot ailanthus trees. Some people call them the "tree of heaven" or the "tree of life." Either name suits me just fine. Yes, we have to keep pulling the small ones out of the adjacent vineyard, but the ones that stay are worth the effort. On a trip east, I was gratified to see these trees, which were introduced to this country by the Chinese during the Gold Rush, now adorning the freeway from Philadelphia to New Jersey.

As I learned from my friend Edward Huntsman-Trout, the brilliant landscape architect, trees have many functions. They provide shade, both to cool and to dapple the ground—and us—with wonderful, dancing shapes. They also break up the skyline in a great variety of patterns. They provide insulation in noisy areas. I understood these functions, and so we planted eight trees in our driveway twenty-three years ago. Only four survived, and those are still quite small, some standing barely twelve feet high. But the trees of heaven, self-sowing and self-sufficient, found the friendliest soil—and prospered.

GROWING IN ONE'S OWN STYLE

Our other very successful, very welcome "gift" tree was a magnificent maple, planted in an area where the children used to play—shading them in the summertime, and now shading their children.

Other tree seedlings constantly appear—live oaks, black oaks, Japanese maples, albizia. If they show up in inappropriate areas, we simply move them carefully into a five-gallon pot and find them a new neighborhood. Often that neighborhood is in one of the grown children's barren gardens. This year, a fig tree decided to present itself right in the orchard. Some time ago, I had planted two fig trees there, and lost them both, despite much love and attention. But this one is thriving, and I have no doubt, since it found its own home, that it will do just fine. Most of the volunteers in our garden were originally invited there by us. But though they didn't end up where we had in mind, ultimately they did just fine. They remind me, yet again, of my children. Like the volunteers, they certainly have minds of their own.

The musician I hoped for became a teacher; the conductor or football player is now in charge of marketing our wines. The opera singer became an artist,

*In the Napa Valley
in early spring, the golden
mustard makes a
glorious background for
the dark trunks of
the grapevine. With plenty
to pick, a large bouquet
is easy.*

*Luke Amaru learning
at an early age to
use the cutting shears.*

the tennis pro a lawyer, the horsewoman a designer, and the writer or philosopher a construction worker. Provided with nourishment and a happy environment, I guess anything will grow, not always the way we plan, but with vigor and beauty.

BEAUTY BEHIND MY BACK

This year, I've spent more time indoors with this book than I have in the garden. But while I've been busy putting words on paper, someone else has been tending the garden—perhaps not exactly in my style, but oh, so beautifully. So many plants appeared of their own volition—feverfew chrysanthemum (*C. parthaneum*), zinnias, cleome, and snapdragons; borage everywhere, arugula here and there, fennel, *salvia sclarea 'turkistanika,'* Johnny-jump-ups, California poppies, lamb's ears, *verbascum bombyciferum*, other mulleins, four-o'clocks, mustard, echium, bachelor's buttons, malvias, and so many more. When I could get outside, to stretch and see what was new, I especially loved the pathway edged with persistent volunteer white feverfew daisies, with their chartreuse foliage against the gray leaves of the blue-purple borage and lacy bronze fennel.

Feverfew, forget-me-nots, borage, and poppies reseed themselves through the planted salvia and iris. As one volunteer completes its bloom, the next fills in, continuously changing the color and pattern of the overgrown areas.

And then there was the sight of Johnny-jump-ups, making a violet carpet under the giant gray-green artichoke leaves. Brilliant California poppies punctuated soft gray lamb's ears (*Stachys lanata*). Several weeks later, the reddish-pink four-o'clocks provided a brilliant rhythm throughout the garden. But perhaps my favorite surprise, the most welcome volunteers, were the larger-than-life artichoke plants springing up right in the middle of a thick field of yellow daffodils. I know it's not quite the scene Wordsworth envisioned, but it was poetry nonetheless.

For sheer drama, there's no volunteer like our Matilija poppies. Originally, we planted five of these tall free-form California and Mexico natives out where they would enjoy full sun, and down below the house, so that we could look down and enjoy their huge white tissue-paper blooms. Now, we have a hundred-foot area, ten feet wide, planted solid with these splendid specimens. When they bloom, I can't tear myself away from them, so I bring them indoors in their full length—eight to nine feet tall. When Martha Stewart first saw them in our entrance hall she thought they were silk. When she realized they were living and breathing, she spent the next two days looking for the seeds or plants to take home to Connecticut. I didn't want to discourage her, but I fear that, like other volunteers, they thrive on neglect, and probably need a longer, hotter growing season than Connecticut provides.

*T*en-foot-tall
Matilija poppies —
Romneya coulteri —
welcome guests as they
enter our home.

*T*he maple leaves outside
and Matilija poppies
inside become one in the
last rays of light.

FORGOTTEN TORTE

This used to be one of my favorite desserts. I could assemble it in ten minutes late at night after I put the children to bed, throw it into the oven, and forget it. Craig Claiborne liked it so much he included it in his New York Times Cook Book, *Volume 4. For a nice sauce, combine sliced fresh peaches or fresh raspberries with a little sugar and Curacao liqueur to taste.*

10 large egg whites
¼ teaspoon cream of tartar
2 cups sugar
1 teaspoon vanilla extract
½ teaspoon almond extract
1 cup whipping cream, whipped and sweetened to taste
Fresh peaches, sliced, or berries

Preheat oven to 450 degrees. Beat egg whites until frothy, then add cream of tartar. Gradually add sugar, beating constantly. Beat in vanilla and almond extracts. Beat until meringue is quite stiff and has a high, glossy sheen.

Spoon meringue into a well-buttered angel food cake pan and smooth with a spoon. Place pan in oven and after five minutes turn oven off. Do not open the oven door for several hours, preferably overnight.

Remove the ragged-looking meringue from the oven. After running a flat blade around the edges, take out center section of the pan.

Don't fret about crust crumbling (you can use crumbs for decorating). Use a spatula to loosen the bottom of the meringue and turn it over onto a large round plate. Cover with sweetened whipped cream. Decorate with leftover crumbled meringue and fresh fruit.

Serves 12 or more

THE BEAUTY OF GROWING OLD

When we let plants go to seed, we see something very special—a cycle we might otherwise miss, and the opportunity to see the plant reproduce itself. As plants start to go to seed, they don't dwindle, shrinking back into themselves. Instead, they reach out, grow tall and thin—growing statelier, and, to my eyes, even more elegant. When I "edit" my volunteers, I rarely have the heart to just yank them out —instead, I find another home for them, somewhere else where I hope they'll flourish.

There's a wonderful messiness, a casual feel to volunteers that softens otherwise rigid lines and borders. It's the naturalness that designer gardens sometimes miss. When violets pop up on the wrong side of a brick border, it's just like introducing an unexpected spice to a soup—it awakens your senses. Nasturtiums are great border-breakers, as that wonderful spilling-over path in Giverny demonstrates.

We have birds and other animals to thank for distributing plants far and wide. Our bed of rockroses (*Cistus*) was given a new start a quarter of a mile away, at the entry to our driveway, thanks to some accommodating bird that had feasted on the berries and then deposited the seeds. I'm glad the bird and the

*The lavender-blue
flowers of borage are a good
contrast to the light blue
of the forget-me-nots and the
chartreuse of the feverfew.*

*Forget-me-nots are
so prolific in early spring that
they are sometimes treated
as a weed. We prefer to honor
them in the living room.*

Cistus got together—I love the look of that strange burnt-pink color, previewing the planted bed well before it comes into view.

At the entrance to the winery, we have a profusion of one particular volunteer most people shun —*Rhus diversiloba*. It's poison oak, and okay, you don't want to lie in it, but without any care at all and not a drop of water all summer *R. diversiloba* provides a lacy green covering under the oaks and madrone, and obligingly turns a beautiful red-orange in the fall.

I've felt a little guilty for most of the year, locked behind my camera or my desk. Fortunately, I had help from Socorro Rodriguez and her father-in-law, Elias, in doing minimal watering (in a drought year) and weeding. I thought the garden would miss my personal involvement. Instead, it's redesigned, reshaped, recolored itself—and I love the surprise and delight of seeing what a finer hand can create. As I relaxed, and saw what wonderful things happened under my neglectful reign this year, I've come to look forward to my garden walks even more than when I fooled myself into thinking I ran the show out there. When I put my pen down, I can't wait to see what's new. I'm never disappointed. And I feel the invitation to come back to work, weed, and play is stronger than ever before. Nature has pushed its way back into our garden and our hearts.

GRACE NOTES FROM THE OAK

Strange how when the children were young I would fend off their endless questions with only half a mind while I was concentrating on the problems at hand. Now, years later, while I'm working on the problems at hand, I'm concentrating on the children, who are no longer children. One of the many parts of gardening that I love is that I can think about other things while I'm making beauty. The parallels between planting and parenting keep coming to mind. If soil is well prepared and enriched before planting, plants grow without much care. Watering and feeding take some practice to know which plants need what care. Plants, like children, are growing, awake or asleep. Winds and storms can shake young plants. So we stake them to help keep them strong. Weeds can be enraging—they take the energy and food a plant needs, and co-opt it for their own. The earlier the weeds are extracted, the less harm they do the neighboring plants. Air is essential to all living things. Children need clean air to breathe, but they also need air in the sense of space to expand. Light is also essential, it can be inspirations or goals to reach for. Plants reach out for it, bask and thrive in it. Plants give us signals. They may start to droop; their leaves lose that glisten. But alert gardeners know the time to intervene is early, before the droop gets more serious. Parenting and planting are both about patience, about being aware—caring, listening, and loving. Just down the path from our house stands a five-hundred-year-old oak, patient and seemingly indestructible. Our children know every branch, every turn, every scar in the trunk of that tree. Though they've been grownup and almost dignified for years, there are still ropes hanging from branches where they played until darkness fell and we ordered them in for dinner. When I was a young mother, I didn't quite appreciate the tree—it was the place I had to go to coax the climbers in, to examine scraped knees, to inquire about chores done—and undone. Now, I often go visit the tree all alone. Sometimes I miss the shrieks, sometimes I revel in the quiet. But I know the tree remembers every giggle, every picnic under its branches, every child who took refuge there with a dog and a book. I look up at the tree, up at the ropes still hanging from its branches, up at the generous green canopy it spreads—and I think, A century from now, someone else will stand here. Whoever she is, whoever he is, the tree connects us, each to the other, and each to the land on Pritchard Hill. This is where the vineyard path inevitably leads me, here to this oak—and to the peace of the garden.

ACKNOWLEDGMENTS

One learns many things when writing a book—about deadlines, production, typesetting, editing, and re-editing, and re-editing, and re-editing—but most of all one learns how important other people are. Most books are a collaboration of sorts, among publisher, designer, writer, editors, and photographers, and ours is no exception.

First of all, Michael Fragnito's joyous enthusiasm about the book when we first met thrilled me and convinced me that Viking Studio Books was the right publisher for us. The kind words of my editor, Barbara Williams, after reading the first section of the book gave me heart. Although our backgrounds and our foot sizes were different, Barbara was somehow able to step into my shoes and edit the book.

Jacqueline Jones and her assistant, Suzie Skugstad, with their beautiful design sense, gave the book real definition and a lovely visual rhythm. Linda Peterson, a warm, bright, and talented woman who is also a parent and loves gardens, was a joy to work with and helped me with the writing. My daughter Lygia, who created the magnificent artwork for the book, also spent hours,

while caring for three small children, helping discuss the direction and the philosophy of the book, as well as helping with the editing. Each of my other children was helpful in his/her own way. Cyril selected slides, Jon-Mark kept bringing me back to reality, Carissa managed to read the entire text while traveling slowly through every state in the Union, and then appeared just in time to help with final editing. Alexa kept encouraging me with fresh ideas, and Dominic's pertinent suggestions in the early drafts were crucial.

Kristin Joyce has a special place on this acknowledgment page, as she showed me that all the time the story was right here on Pritchard Hill beneath my feet, "A Footpath Through Our Garden."

Books don't happen in a few weeks or even months. I must give James Beard credit, for it was he and M. F. K. Fisher who many years ago began prodding me to put Pritchard Hill into a book. Judith Jones, the senior editor at Knopf who was sent by James Beard to Pritchard Hill, was especially encouraging, giving me tips on writing and sending books to inspire me. Bonnie Predd and Deborah Rabin

saw something early on in a first draft that others couldn't see.

Many writers gave me helpful suggestions along the way—Nancy Powers, Sharon Wick, Diane Saeks, Sally Belk, Priscilla Dunhill, and special cooking friends Marion Cunningham and Jimmy Dodge.

The enthusiasm and guidance of Chris Tomasino, my agent, has been invaluable. Judith Applebaum, codirector of Sensible Solution, provided a positive attitude and keen direction in the early stages.

Most of the photography was done on Pritchard Hill, but occasionally we shot elsewhere and I wish to thank the people who so graciously invited us into their homes—Lynsay and Michael Harrison, Chotsie Blanc, Susan Robbins, Bob and Alex Phillips, Elaine Cunningham. Sara Slavin, who produced the beautiful book On Flowers, was helpful in giving ideas from the very beginning and ended up helping style many of the photos for us.

Very important members of the computer, slide sorting, and editorial staff were Jane O'Neil, Jan Schaefer, Caryn Reading, Andrea Rossman,

Tiffany Murray, Jeri Bernier, Colleen McGlinn, Ann Cutting, who also helped tend my garden, and Michele Forrest.

Friends who were most giving of their time and talents were Don and Sue Meredith, Anne Marie Cordingly, Joan Westgate, Margrit Biever, Virginia Van Asperin, Robbie Deane, Susanne Brangham, Susan Robbins, Patty Skouras, Mary Nell McCann, Jan Sterling, Mary Trotter, Lisa Larson, Cyndacy Kaudris, Dave Perio, our viticulturist, Glenn Janss, and Sarah Hammond. My sister Jayne Unander, Virginia Wolff of Virginia Wolff Floral Designs, Chicago, and Marjorie Eckels read the entire text and provided extremely helpful comments. Marjorie's energy and devotion for the past ten years has been invaluable.

A very special thanks to two associates in my company, Artforms, the late and very talented Larry Stripling, who left us much too early, and to Alice Jones, whose talents are as big as her heart. I'd like to mention just a few of our many wonderful clients who have given us an opportunity to stretch our imaginations: John Loder at KQED, the American Institute of Wine and Food, Cranberry Ocean

Spray, James Nassikas and Gerald Asher, Martha May, Sally Debenham, Kay Woods, and LaLou Bize LeRoy of Romanée-Conti.

Socorro Rodriguez is responsible for keeping me sane and adding joy and beauty to my life. Luanne and Frank Wells have done more than they know to make the book possible.

The list of gratitudes would be surely lacking if it did not include parents. Although it was my father who was more of a philosopher, poet, and artist, it was my practical and wise mother who gave me the task of setting the tables and decorating for special occasions. The sister of my father, dear Aunt Blue, taught us about fantasy and make-believe. The constant support from Donn's father was always encouraging. From his mother, I keep learning about beauty and about composting and, I hope, how to stay young at heart.

And last, but not least, a soft-spoken, incredible person, Donn, the father of all six children, who manages to see clearly and keep his humor and a proper perspective no matter how many rooms I take over with my papers and layouts, and no matter what chaos reigns.

PHOTO CREDITS

One of the most enjoyable parts of this book was photographing it, whether personally or in conjunction with a talented photographer. Sharing the excitement of a particular view, the light, or a detail added greatly to the joy of recording scenes on Pritchard Hill. I am enormously grateful to each and every photographer I worked with, and only wish I had not been so busy scouting out the next location or preparing a set-up or lunch and could have taken notes from their tremendous knowledge. I found that most photographers are like gardeners—they are generous, giving, enthusiastic people. I thank you all.

I particularly want to thank some who spent a bit more time on Pritchard Hill. First of all, going back 15 years, there's Peter Aaron, who was originally sent here from New York for a story, then came back to help shoot the book. An association with Michael Landis and Daniel D'Agostini began years ago when photographing for a book was only a fantasy, but their talents and photos were real. Susan and Joseph Woods, both excellent landscape photographers, made themselves available at critical times. It was a

delight to work with Michael Lamotte, who knows more about still-life photography than anyone in the world. And, finally, Gretta Mitchell, an artist and mother, was willing to try anything to get the effects we wanted.

Peter Aaron
vi, 12-13, 44-45, 51, 70, 70-71, 120-21, 132-33, 146, 146-47, 170, 206-7, 240-41, 250-51, 252-53, 256-57, 286-87

Bill Apton
258

Frank Balthis
54-55, 64-65, 89

John Blaustein
14-15, 58, 79, 207, 275, 283

Craig Buchanan
126, 127

Molly Chappellet
6, 8-9, 10-11, 16-17, 20, 21, 24-25, 26-27, 30-31, 34-35, 38, 42-43, 48-49, 56-57, 62, 62-63, 68-69, 72-73, 76, 78-79, 80, 82-83, 84-85, 86-87, 88-89, 90-91, 92-93, 94-95, 96-97, 98, 98-99, 100-1, 108, 112-13, 115, 124-25, 130-31, 140-41, 142-43, 144-45, 148, 150-51, 154, 156-57, 158-59, 160, 160-61, 164-65, 168-69, 170-71, 172-73, 188-89, 192, 194-95, 201, 204-5, 209, 212-13, 218-19, 220-21, 230, 234-

35, 236-37, 242-43, 246, 254-55, 257, 260-61, 264-65, 268, 270-71, 272-73, 274-75, 280-81, 282-83, 289

Daniel D'Agostini
22-23, 26, 50-51, 54, 110-11, 114-15, 136-37, 137, 138-39, 166-67, 198-99, 208, 220, 235

John Dominis
128-29

Kathryn Kleinman
All photos of paintings by Lygia Chappellet

Michael Lamotte
29, 81, 148-49, 165, 166, 174, 175, 176-77, 178, 178-79, 180, 181, 182-83

Michael Landis
184-85, 248-49, 263

Thomas Lea
134-35

Brian Leatart
186-87, 262-63

Fred Lyon
v, 258-59

Bill Miller
118-19

Margaretta Mitchell
x, 15, 18, 19, 28, 32, 33, 46-47, 47, 52-53, 59, 60-61, 65, 66, 67, 162-63, 196-97, 200, 202-3, 210, 210-11, 215, 216-17, 217, 222-23, 232-33, 238, 239, 241, 276-77, 278, 279, 284-85

Fran Ortiz
141

Earl Roberge
134

Doug Sterling
139

Ted Streshinsky
122-23

Joseph Woods
53, 116-17, 130